ISBN 0

WHY THE CHURCH?

WHY THE CHURCH?

edited by
Walter J. Burghardt, S.J.
and
William G. Thompson, S.J.

Contributors

J. Peter Schineller, S.J.

Eugene A. LaVerdiere, S.S.S.

William G. Thompson, S.J.

J. Patout Burns, S.J.

Roger D. Haight, S.J.

Robert T. Sears, S.J.

PAULIST PRESS
New York/Ramsey/Toronto

Library of Congress
Catalog Card Number: 77-74583

ISBN: 0-8091-2028-3

Published by Paulist Press
Editorial Office: 1865 Broadway, N.Y., N.Y. 10023
Business Office: 545 Island Road, Ramsey, N.J. 07446

Printed and bound in the
United States of America

CONTENTS

PREFACE

The need for collaboration in theology is now recognized as a crucial one by theologians of every persuasion. Whether articulated in demanding methodological terms by Bernard Lonergan or more simply experienced as the need to consult with one's colleagues, the call for collaboration now meets widespread acceptance.

However, most of us rarely have the opportunity to study the results of serious and sustained collaboration in theology. The present book, originally a special issue of the journal *Theological Studies* (December 1976), will prove, I believe, a sure remedy for that lack. After reading these articles individually, the reader will note the consistent cross-references, the forthrightness in stating with clarity both significant differences and similarities (especially in the articles by Roger D. Haight and Robert T. Sears). Then the reader may well experience, as I did, a sense of exhilaration that here the fruits of serious collaboration among several specialists with sometimes different, sometimes identical, theological viewpoints are readily available. For these articles do not represent a new "school" of theology, nor are they merely another "special issue" of all-too-individual articles on a common theme. Rather, these articles represent the fruits of a serious effort at collaboration in theology by six members of the faculty of the Jesuit School of Theology in Chicago. Each author read and criticized the earlier versions of the articles of his colleagues. Moreover, as the consistently high level of theological argument demonstrates, that mutual criticism helped each author sharpen his own criteria, warrants, backings, and argument in accord with both the demands of his own discipline and the demands of the results of his colleagues.

On methodological grounds, therefore, this work strikes me as possessing singular importance for all theologians. For there remains no greater need for theology today than to assure that it function as a genuinely collaborative discipline. There are, alas, all too few models at hand to demonstrate the results of such collaboration. One hopes

PREFACE

that this book may encourage all of us to enter into fuller collaborative efforts with our colleagues.

To emphasize the methodological contribution of this volume, however, should not detract from the importance of the substantive theological issues at stake. Fortunately, relatively little need be said on this aspect, since the articles speak clearly and forcefully for themselves. However, it may prove useful to note certain factors which at least one reader found particularly helpful in the substantive discussion on ecclesiology.

Indeed, the clarification of the central issues of contemporary ecclesiology by a deliberate initial choice of subject matters for investigation seems exemplary here. The need to develop some basic typologies on really distinct ecclesiologies and each one's relationship to a Christology is obvious. The article by J. Peter Schineller, proposing four types of ecclesiology and Christology, demonstrates the fruitfulness of all careful typological analysis: illumination of increasingly complex material by signalizing basic differences and basic similarities in really distinct positions on fundamental theological questions.

The choice of historical materials for investigation seems equally appropriate. The choice of the Matthean and Lukan ecclesiologies for contemporary study, for example—rather than the Pauline and Johannine—is argued by Eugene A. LaVerdiere and William G. Thompson on persuasive grounds: precisely as communities in notable and distinct transition periods of the Church's life, the Matthean and Lukan ecclesiologies clarify our present ecclesial situation in unexpected ways. By analyzing both the context-dependent and context-transcendent factors in the ecclesiologies of the redactors of Matthew and Luke-Acts, the authors show their readers how these scriptural texts can play an appropriately normative role for contemporary Christian theology.

The choice of Gregory of Nyssa and Augustine for the patristic period by J. Patout Burns is argued for on equally persuasive grounds. Moreover, Fr. Burns's unusual ability to employ both exegetical and typological methods in his analysis provides his article with a hermeneutical method that renders the complex ecclesiologies of those two masters, Augustine and Gregory, surprisingly clear rather than unnecessarily complicated or *simpliste*.

Finally, the two contemporary, constructive theological articles by Roger Haight and Robert Sears provide the reader with the unusual service of finding two major and distinct options for contemporary ecclesiology spelled out in a manner both deliberate and original. The forceful and carefully-argued manner by which each author articulates his ecclesiology enlightens the contemporary discussion by signalizing the theologically significant similarities and differences between a "mission" ecclesiology and a "community" ecclesiology. The authors share a passion for raising the more usual discussions of "social action" and/or "spirituality" to an authentically theological level wherein one sees that one's very understanding of "church" is at stake. Each shares, as well, a drive to articulate not only his own position but the strengths and weaknesses of major contemporary alternatives. Whether —more exactly, how far—these positions are complementary or divergent, each reader must judge for her/himself.

In the meantime, this volume should aid all readers to sharpen their theological understanding on both methodological and substantive issues. For so rare a combination of collaborative skills and substantive results the editor of *Theological Studies,* Walter J. Burghardt, S.J., and the authors deserve the admiration of us all. The issues at stake are so central to any Christian theologian that one may be sure that a critical conversation in several quarters will ensue. Thereby the wider ongoing collaboration which the authors have initiated will surely continue.

David Tracy
Divinity School, University of Chicago

I

CHRIST AND CHURCH: A SPECTRUM OF VIEWS

J. PETER SCHINELLER, S.J.

Jesuit School of Theology in Chicago

REFERRING TO the present state of Catholicism, Langdon Gilkey writes: "Aggiornamento thus poses a quite new and much deeper problem: not what form of Catholicism [contemporary Catholics] will or wish to live within, but whether they wish to be Catholic or Christian at all."[1] He then expands his remark in a footnote, describing conversations with Catholic students and seminarians. At first the questions relate to how to reinterpret Catholic belief and identity, so as to be in harmony with modernity. But then, Gilkey adds, the more ultimate questions always appear: Why should we be Catholics or Christians at all, and not just humanistic and secular?[2] Clearly this type of questioning indicates a shift in the type of self-examination among Catholics today.

A similar way of seeing this shift might be found in the following suggested characterization of three phases in American Catholic attitudes. From the time of Vatican II until the present, the doctrine of the anonymous Christian has gained widespread familiarity and acceptance. In place of a Roman Church as the exclusive way of salvation, we begin to appreciate the grace-filled insights and experiences of non-Catholics. Yet we still interpret their experience in terms of our own Christian perspective. More recently we have entered a second and confusing phase, where we are re-examining our universal claims and, together with this, our self-identity as Christians. We ask: Why is a Christian Church or community necessary if God's salvific grace is available for all? Why any missionary effort?[3] Perhaps a third phase, insofar as we have made progress in resolving the tensions of the previous phase, is this: Granted that God's love and grace is available to all, what is our distinct contribution to the human community as Christians? Is there mutual enrichment in the examination of the claims and actual life-style of Christians and non-Christians?

The cause of this new type of questioning referred to by Gilkey and experienced by Christians today seems to be the new context in which Christians must live. It is no longer possible (if it ever was) to live as a Christian, or to do Christian theology, without considering the questions

---

[1] Langdon Gilkey, *Catholicism Confronts Modernity* (New York, 1975) p. 42.

[2] *Ibid.*, p. 205.

[3] The question of the mission and goal of the Church will be taken up in the subsequent essays, especially those by Haight and Sears, exemplifying two different approaches and viewpoints.

1

asked of the Christian, and claims made, by non-Christians. When these questions and claims enter deeply into our framework of living and thinking, they cause us to examine our theological stances. Many of the older theories and positions simply do not fit the new experiences, and adjustments must be made.

Thus the problematic context for our discussion must be the Church in the modern world, or Christ and contemporary culture. The context is not an in-Church horizon, nor is it a secular-humanist horizon. It is precisely in the correlation of the two, in the recognition that the Church is in the world and the world in the Church, in the recognition that Christ and the Christian are always related to culture and influenced by it. The forces that affect our theologizing are as much outside as inside the Church.[4]

Indications of this are found in several recent theological trends: secular city, death of God, theology of hope, civil religions, liberation theology. In each of these we see an opening of the Christian problematic to data and forces from non-Christian sources. The theological discussion takes its problematic not so much from the horizon of thinkers such as Barth and Bultmann, but from the questions raised by theologians such as Troeltsch, Bonhoeffer, and Tillich in their continued questioning of the very foundations of Christian theology in relation to culture, social contexts, and the general history of religions.

We have been forced to move, as Rahner suggests, towards an open Catholicism, in dialogue not only with non-Catholic Christians but with non-Christians and even anti-Christians.[5] In this coming to terms with the experience of modernity there have been reactions at both ends of the spectrum, right and left, liberal and conservative. Furthermore, I suggest that fundamental questions are involved in this encounter with modernity, questions of Christology and ecclesiology. An examination of the responses of Christians today to basic questions—"who is the Christ?" and "why the Church?"—would unearth a wide range of substantive differences.

In an attempt to sort out these differences and to shed light on the problematic facing Christianity today, I will set forth a spectrum of four views in Christology and ecclesiology. The spectrum of positions may seem blunt and too sharp at first glance, but it does pose in stark terms the options we face. The goal of the presentation of the four views is

[4] This point is developed in Haight's essay, in the early section entitled "The Church as Problem."

[5] Rahner employs the phrase "open Catholicism" at the very beginning of one of his more important essays, "Christianity and Non-Christian Religions," *Theological Investigations* 5 (Baltimore, 1966) 115.

basically expository rather than critical, leading to self-understanding and exploration rather than aiming for closure or a decided option among positions. But before we set forth the four positions, some preliminary comments on the type of views we present must be given.

CHARACTERISTICS OF THE SPECTRUM

Before describing positively what the spectrum consists of, I note two examples of models which it is not. It is not a duplication of the classic work of H. Richard Niebuhr, *Christ and Culture*.[6] His five types focus on the relation of Christ and culture. While mine necessarily include that question, they focus more directly on the place and necessity of Christ and the Church for the salvation of mankind. In addition, in his models the positive or negative factors present in a particular culture or situation would partially determine how Christ would interact with that situation. Secondly, my spectrum is not like the five models of Church presented by Avery Dulles in his important *Models of the Church*.[7] His models are primarily descriptive, image-related models that point to the reality of the Church. They are complementary rather than exclusive. That is to say, a complete view of the Church would involve elements of the Church as institutional, sacramental, communitarian, kerygmatic, and servant.

In the spectrum I am setting forth, the four views are intentionally designed to be mutually exclusive rather than complementary. Logically, you cannot hold two of them. They might be termed systematic models rather than descriptive, and they will refer to views that would be considered unorthodox as well as orthodox. Clearly they are not sociological models, gained from a survey of the attitudes of Christians. They are theological, and are constructed methodically to explore the different logical possibilities of professing one's faith in Jesus as the Christ. The key words that distinguish one position from the next are carefully chosen precisely in order to make the logical and theological distinctiveness of the positions sharp and clear, and not merely to indicate shades of difference. Because of these differences in substance, if

---

[6] New York, 1961. Charles Davis, *Christ and the World Religions* (London, 1970), adapts the five types of Niebuhr to the problem of Christ and world religions. While this is illuminating, it is different from my task, which is to focus directly on the indispensability of Christ for salvation. Most helpful for my discussion of types and models is the second chapter of David Tracy's *Blessed Rage for Order* (New York, 1975). He presents five methodological models in contemporary theology, which often intersect with our spectrum. But here, too, he focuses upon method and presuppositions, while my direct focus is on the Christological and ecclesiological content. Tracy's footnotes (esp. p. 34, n. 1) present bibliographical references on the use of types and models.

[7] New York, 1974. Dulles' introduction and first chapter present a rationale for the use of models in ecclesiology.

you choose one position on the spectrum, you cannot hold any of the others at the same time.[8]

An additional way of viewing this spectrum is by seeing it as a functional approach to Christology and ecclesiology. I am presenting four exclusive, noncomplementary positions on the extent to which Jesus Christ is Savior for all mankind. I am not examining his inner self or person, or even the manner in which he redeems mankind. So, too, in regard to ecclesiology, I am not describing or defining the Church in terms of its inner principle of unity, but in terms of its function in and for the world.

While Catholic theologians would probably set themselves in the middle of the spectrum, avoiding the extremes of right and left, the advantage of the full spectrum is that it points out extremes to be avoided, extremes which in curious and subtle ways influence our thought and conduct. We live in an age of pluralism, including theological pluralism within the Church. In this situation the clear and distinct boundaries between orthodoxy and heterodoxy are not always clearly distinguishable. Thus, Rahner in an essay on heresy speaks of the presence and danger of latent heresies and leanings to heresy that might affect the theologian.[9] While these inclinations remain unarticulated, they do affect our spontaneous practice and our response in dialogue, even if they are screened out in more reflective theological writings or lectures. In an analogy from moral theology, we can speak of a core vs. a peripheral systematic theology. What we say and hold in the core of our Christian existence may be orthodox, but that could be surrounded and influenced by attitudes, instincts, or customs that might be unorthodox. We must accordingly be alert to inconsistencies between our theory and practice. A theoretical commitment to Jesus as the Christ, as the way, truth, and life, could well be in tension with our lived practice and practical attitude towards nonbelievers. So, too, while in theory we see the Church as the light of nations, in practice we could too easily settle for an attitude of practical indifferentism.

In addition, theologians must constantly strive for internal consistency. That is to say, a position in Christology must be theologically consistent with the necessarily related positions of sin, grace, faith, and Trinity. In examining and working towards such consistency, the presentation of a spectrum of views can be of considerable assistance. At the end of this essay I will point beyond Christology and ecclesiology to

[8] While the spectrum presents four positions that are mutually exclusive, the theologian will probably find himself inclining or moving from his own position towards neighboring positions.

[9] Karl Rahner, *On Heresy* (New York, 1964). See, e.g., pp. 23–24, 37–38, 48–49. He employs the term "latent heresy" throughout.

other related areas of theology exemplified by the four positions on the spectrum.

In setting forth this spectrum of views, I am necessarily inadequate to the detailed analyses and distinctions that could be made within each position. And when I refer to specific theologians, this is done not to place them squarely in one or other position, but to exemplify the position I am presenting. It must also be admitted that the spectrum is inadequate to the differences that exist between Christian Churches. For my purposes, I include under "Christian Church" the mainline Churches, that would hold to belief in Jesus as the Christ, as Lord and Savior, and would exercise the sacraments of baptism and the Lord's Supper. I take the liberty of speaking in broad strokes of the Christian Churches, since the focal point of this essay is more upon the forces from outside affecting the Churches than the differences between Christian communities.

The reason why I set forth a Christological position first, and then the related ecclesiology, is a theological one. Even though ecclesiology has been in the center of Roman Catholic theology since Vatican II, I maintain that an ecclesiology follows from more basic positions taken (implicitly or explicitly) in Christology. The function and mission of the Church follows from the function and mission of Christ.[10] In presenting the four positions, I begin with the most conservative and move towards the most liberal. The order could readily have been reversed. In fact, for the spectrum to function as an aid to the self-understanding of the theologian, it would be valuable to view one's own position from both directions, that is, as moving both towards and away from the more liberal and conservative positions.

Finally, I mention briefly what is common to all four views. In terms of Christology, all affirm that Jesus Christ is *a* way to salvation, a mediator of authentic existence. All view the Church as *a* way or means to salvation. They differ, however, on the relation of Jesus to other mediators of salvation, and on the relation of the Church to other mediations. They differ, therefore, on the degree of dispensability and the normative value of Jesus Christ and the Church for salvation. Salvation I am interpreting in a broad sense to mean God's activity whereby mankind is delivered from sin and its consequences. The saved person lives in accord with the reign of God, beginning in this life and achieving its fulness in life everlasting. The gifts and fruits of the Spirit as described by Paul characterize this saved life.[11]

[10] Each of the following essays will in different ways test and verify this principle–in the scriptural evidence, in patristic thought, and in contemporary theology of the Church.

[11] I do not enter into the complex question of the meaning of salvation as interior/spiritual vs. external/developmental. While this discussion, especially among theologies of liberation, is central to theology today, it is not the focus of my concern.

FIGURE 1

A SPECTRUM OF CHRISTOLOGIES AND ECCLESIOLOGIES

I Ecclesiocentric universe, exclusive Christology

Jesus Christ and Church constitutive and exclusive way of salvation

God's saving grace → Jesus Christ → explicit Church only

II Christocentric universe, inclusive Christology

a) Jesus Christ and Church constitutive but not exclusive way of salvation

God's saving grace → Jesus Christ → explicit Church → all humanity

b) Jesus Christ constitutive but Church nonconstitutive way of salvation

God's saving grace → Jesus Christ ⟨ explicit Church / all humanity

III Theocentric universe, normative Christology

Jesus Christ and Church normative but not constitutive way of salvation

God's saving grace ⟨ Jesus Christ as normative → Church / various religions, all humanity

IV Theocentric universe, nonnormative Christology

Jesus Christ one of many ways of salvation

God's saving grace ⟨ Jesus Christ → Church / various religions, all humanity

A brief view of Figure I will provide an overview of where I am moving. I will analyze each of the four positions in detail, beginning with the first.

ECCLESIOCENTRIC UNIVERSE, EXCLUSIVE CHRISTOLOGY

Christology

The first position on the spectrum is the most conservative. It maintains that there are no other mediators of salvation than Jesus, since he is the only God-willed revealer of God's grace and salvation. All other savior figures are idols, man-created, with no power to lead to salvation. It is only through explicit personal knowledge of and commitment to Jesus as the Christ that salvation is possible. Jesus becomes a mediator of salvific grace only through a personal relationship to him. In other words, the activity of the divine Logos is limited to those who have explicit contact with the life and teaching of Jesus of Nazareth. In this position the universe could be considered as Christocentric, and in an exclusive sense. Jesus Christ is the center and key to the meaning of human existence, and he becomes this for the individual only insofar as the individual comes to explicit awareness of, and contact with, Christ.

In the course of Christian history, scriptural evidence for this position has been found in texts such as these: "There is no other name in the whole world given to man by which we are to be saved" (Acts 4:12); "He who believes and is baptized will be saved; but he who does not believe will be condemned" (Mk 16:15–16); "Without me you can do nothing" (Jn 15:5); "I am the way, the truth, and the life. No one comes to the Father except through me" (Jn 14:6).

Ecclesiology

The normal corollary to such a strict Christological position is a literalist interpretation of the maxim "Outside the Church no salvation." Because of its close connection with the saving events of the life of Jesus, the Church (as Christ) is the exclusive institution of salvation. The individual attains salvation only through explicit membership in the Church, since there is no other mediator of the salvation of Christ. Other religions, just as other savior figures, are false—fascinating but futile human attempts to reach the one and true God who is revealed exclusively in Christ. Scriptural evidence for this ecclesiological position is found in the missionary command at the end of Matthew's Gospel[12] and in the baptismal and Eucharistic texts of John's Gospel: "Unless a man is born through water and the Spirit, he cannot enter the kingdom of God" (Jn 3:5); and "If you do not eat the flesh of the Son of Man and

---

[12] For an exegetical interpretation of these texts of Matthew, see the section of Thompson's essay on "The Gentile Mission."

drink his blood, you will not have life in you" (Jn 6:53). In this first position, therefore, there is no grace in the world if there is no Church.

Elements of this position are found in some explanations of infant baptism, in discussions of Limbo, and in some explanations of the missionary thrust of the Church. It helped account for the strong and tenacious missionary stance of saints such as Francis Xavier. Baptism is considered the necessary means to avoid eternal condemnation. Jansenism reflects this position in its rigor, and Leonard Feeney, of the more recent past, also exemplified it.[13]

In summary, this ecclesiological position is even more rigorous than an exclusive Christocentric view. It results in an ecclesiocentric universe.[14]

CHRISTOCENTRIC UNIVERSE, INCLUSIVE CHRISTOLOGY

Christology

If the first position could be characterized as an exclusive ecclesiocentric position, then this position is an inclusive Christocentric position. Since this and the following view of the spectrum seem to be most widely held and thus at the center of theological discussions today, I will present them in greater detail.

The second position is less rigorist than the first insofar as it moves from an exclusive view of Christ and the Church to one that allows for anonymous or implicit Christian faith as a way to salvation. It is more optimistic about the possibility of salvation. While persons can only be saved by the grace of Christ, that grace is offered and available to all, even to those who have never heard of Jesus of Nazareth. In this emphasis it is in sharp contrast to the previous position. In its positive tenets it maintains that there is only one economy of salvation, that Jesus Christ is the normative revelation of God and is constitutive of the work of God in the world. He is the mediator of all other revelations, and the salvation which can be attained in the world first occurs in Jesus and occurs elsewhere only through him.

The key word that distinguishes this position from the following is "constitutive."[15] To say that Jesus is the constitutive mediator of

[13] Catholic magisterial statements condemning heretical aspects of Jansenism can be found in Denzinger-Schönmetzer: e.g., 1295 (2305).

[14] Pertinent here is Hans Küng's essay "The World Religions in God's Plan of Salvation," in *Christian Revelation and World Religions*, ed. Josef Neuner (London, 1967). He discusses the history and meaning of the phrase "Outside the Church no salvation," and shows it to be an ecclesiocentric view of the universe.

[15] I have chosen the word "constitutive" to specifically characterize this second position of the spectrum. Other words have been employed by systematic theologians to indicate this type of high Christology: e.g., Jesus Christ as the absolute, final, unsurpassable, irrevocable, universal, eschatological, definitive, and unique mediator of salvation. Without examining them, we can see that they point to a common theme, signifying the essential constitutive function and importance of Jesus Christ for the salvation of mankind.

salvation is to say that he is not only normative but the indispensable one. Without him there would be no salvation. He is the efficient cause or the condition apart from which there would be no saving grace in the world. The name "*Jesus* Christ" indicates that this saving event is constituted not by the eternal Logos but only because the Logos became flesh in Jesus of Nazareth. "Constitutive," therefore, means that without this historical incarnation, life, death, and resurrection, no person would be saved.

To explain how the saving grace of Christ is present and operative beyond the explicit Christian pale, theologians speak of the anonymous Christian, the latent Church, and the supernatural existential. In these moves, the second position is clearly distinguished from the previous. Salvation is here available *extra Christum*, but it is only possible *propter Christum*.

Two key scriptural texts for this position are 1 Tim 2:4–6, "God our Savior desires all men to be saved and to come to the knowledge of the truth; for there is one God and there is one mediator between God and man, the man Jesus Christ, who gave himself as a ransom for all"; and Acts 17:23, where Paul says that what the Athenians worship as unknown, he proclaims to them in proclaiming Jesus Christ as risen Lord. Rahner, for example, relies heavily upon these texts in speaking of God's universal salvific will.[16]

Jesus remains the center, not only decisively revealing, but also constituting and making available, God's love to all mankind. He is the condition apart from which we cannot achieve authentic existence and salvation. It is only in and through Jesus that God's salvific will becomes operative in human history. Thus Rahner, for example, writes in his key essay on Christianity and non-Christian religions that "God desires the salvation of everyone; and this salvation willed by God is the salvation won by Christ."[17] He exemplifies what we mean by "constitutive" when he writes: "He namely, as God made man, is the true and only efficient cause of our salvation; as Son of God he is our salvation itself, and access of grace to God the Father."[18] From its very inception, God's plan to save all mankind has proceeded from the God-man as its starting point and to him as its goal.

Ecclesiology

In this as in the first position, Jesus is the constitutive, normative mediator of God's salvation to mankind. But divergences from the first

---

[16] Among the many places where Rahner employs these texts, see the clear statement in his *The Christian of the Future* (New York, 1967) pp. 94–97.

[17] *Art. cit.* (n. 5 above) p. 122.

[18] Karl Rahner, *Mary, Mother of the Lord* (New York, 1963) p. 95.

position appear clearly when we move from Christology to ecclesiology. There is a decisive move away from the narrow and literalist interpretation of the maxim "Outside the Church no salvation." One does not have to be explicitly Christian to be saved, even though those not explicitly Christian are saved only through the grace of Christ that is manifest and present in the Church today.

This ecclesiological position finds echoes in the documents of Vatican II. For example, the Dogmatic Constitution on the Church speaks of those who can be saved if they sincerely seek God and follow the dictates of their conscience. In a footnote the document refers to the letter from the Holy See to Cardinal Cushing opposing the position of Leonard Feeney on the salvation of non-Christians. A parallel position is found in the Constitution on the Church in the Modern World.[19] While this second position is clear in that we can be saved without becoming explicit members of the Church, what is not entirely clear is whether the Church must be viewed as the constitutive mediator of the salvific grace of God to mankind. Hence we must examine two possibilities for an ecclesiology; (a) the Church as the constitutive mediator of grace, just as Jesus Christ is constitutive mediator, and (b) the Church as not a constitutive mediator of grace, but representing or pointing to the constitutive mediation of Christ.

a) Because of a close and inseparable link between Christ and the Church, the grace of Christ becomes available to non-Christians only through the Church. That is to say, if the Church were to cease, so would the salvific grace of Christ. The Church is as much a necessary mediator of grace as Christ himself is, and is indispensable for the salvation of mankind. The maxim "Outside the Church no salvation" comes to mean "Without the Church no salvation." If there is no Church in the world, then there is no salvation.[20] A scriptural text exemplifying this position would be the words of Jesus, "He who hears you hears me, and he who rejects you rejects me" (Lk 10:16). So, too, the image of the body of Christ employed by Paul indicates that separation from the body necessarily involves separation from the head, Jesus Christ.

Two references to theologians are added, to exemplify this position in ecclesiology. De Lubac, among his powerful and beautiful writings on the Church, expresses himself as follows:

[19] Dogmatic Constitution on the Church, no. 16 (*The Documents of Vatican II*, ed. W. M. Abbott [New York, 1966] p. 35); Pastoral Constitution on the Church in the Modern World, no. 22 (pp. 221–22).

[20] Heinz Robert Schlette, in his *Towards a Theology of Religions* (New York, 1966), explains that this interpretation of the maxim is substantially held by Michael Schmaus; see p. 16.

if . . . the formula "Outside the Church no salvation" has still an ugly sound, there is no reason why it should not be put in a positive form and read, appealing to all men of good will, not "Outside the Church you are damned," but "It is by the Church and by the Church alone that you will be saved." For it is through the Church that salvation will come, that it is already coming to mankind.[21]

Rahner writes in similar vein that "It is only in Jesus Christ that this salvation is conferred, and through Christianity and the one Church that it must be mediated to all men."[22]

b) In the second type of ecclesiology, the Church is viewed as the representative community in continuity with Christ. Because of this closeness to Christ, the Church is a privileged mediator of salvation. Yet, because the work of Christ has been accomplished and his Spirit given, even if the Church were to cease, God's salvific grace won by Christ would remain present and effective. The maxim "Outside the Church no salvation" in this position indicates that the Church signifies or points to the reality of God's salvation operative throughout the world.[23] While the Church mediates this salvation to its own members, it serves only to point non-Christians to the reality of God's grace that has always been present and available.

The Church's mission here is not one of absolute necessity of survival, in order that God's grace may be present, but a mission to represent and proclaim the love of God which is operative and available to all. In making the love of God more explicit by witnessing to its fullest manifestation in Christ Jesus, the Church makes a fuller and more explicit living of the saved life possible. Walter Kasper speaks along these lines: "The Church's mission, which is rooted in the absolute claim of Christianity, is not so much to save the individual—who in principle can be saved outside its visible communion—as to represent and proclaim the love of God, to give testimony to hope, and so to be a sign among the nations."[24] In accord with this position, to be saved, a non-Christian need not necessarily have a desire for the Church (*votum ecclesiae*), only a desire for Christ (*votum implicitum Christi*).

THEOCENTRIC UNIVERSE, NORMATIVE CHRISTOLOGY

Christology

If the previous position is best characterized as an inclusive Chris-

[21] Henri de Lubac, *Catholicism* (New York, 1950) p. 118.

[22] Karl Rahner, "The Church, Churches, and Religions," *Theological Investigations* 10 (New York, 1973) 31.

[23] An example of this interpretation can be found in the essay on Church in *Sacramentum mundi* 1, in the subsection entitled "Outside the Church No Salvation," by Marie-Joseph LeGuillou.

[24] Walter Kasper, "Absoluteness of Christianity," in *Sacramentum mundi* 1, 312.

tocentric view, this might be called a theocentric position, with Jesus as the normative expression of the loving and salvific nature of God. While the key word of the previous position was "constitutive," here the key word is "normative." We can unpack its meaning by beginning with a standard definition, where a norm is a rule or authoritative standard. The word is familiar to Christian theologians from its application to Scripture as the *norma normans, non normata* for Christian theology. It indicates, therefore, a measurer, a superior or ideal type, which can function to measure, correct, and judge others by its own standard or correct measure. When applied to the person and work of Jesus Christ, "normative" indicates that he is the revelation and mediation from God which corrects and fulfils all other mediations. It does not imply that he is the constitutive, unique, or unsurpassable mediator of salvation for all mankind.

It is important to note that this third position presents a real option between the second and fourth positions. If we cannot affirm Jesus Christ as constitutive mediator, we do not necessarily shift to a position of total relativity. There is a middle position, where the key concept of normativeness enters.

What reasons move theologians from the Christocentric to the theocentric view, where Jesus remains highly significant, as the normative mediator of God's saving grace? As the Christian theologian becomes more aware of the positive values of other religions, he begins to examine more carefully the uniqueness and universality of his own claims. So, too, the *de facto* minority status of Christians is seen as a given that will not be overcome in the foreseeable future. If God desires all to be saved, much of His saving activity will be accomplished in a religious milieu which is non-Christian. The very fact that several theologians begin to speak of Christianity as the extraordinary way of salvation, and of other religions as the ordinary way, indicates a shift in perspective.[25]

In a more directly theological line of argument, the danger of the previous position is that it can tend to equate theology with Christology in an unnuanced manner. It inclines to a position where we say that God has never spoken to man at all except in the incarnation of Jesus of Nazareth. Jesus becomes the constitutive mediator not only of salvation but of all human knowledge and truth. H. Richard Niebuhr thus explains that by inclining to substitute Christology for theology, we incline to substitute the love of Jesus Christ for the love of God.[26] The previous

[25] See, e.g., the works of Hans Küng and Heinz Robert Schlette already cited (nn. 14 and 20 above).

[26] Niebuhr expresses this caution in *The Purpose of the Church and its Ministry* (New York, 1956) pp. 44 ff.

position, in addition, has difficulty in accounting for the reality of man's life with God prior to the historical appearance of Jesus of Nazareth. To maintain its strong Christocentric focus, it speaks of a proleptic appropriation of his benefits, or the anticipated merits of Christ affecting persons born before the saving action of Jesus. By this move it avoids the obvious difficulty of affirming that God was unforgiving until Christ came.

Viewed positively, this third Christological position states that Jesus Christ is the normative way to God and His salvation, but he is neither the exclusive nor the constitutive way. Salvation, which was always possible for all mankind, becomes decisively and normatively manifest in Jesus. God is love, and this love has been operative always and everywhere; this love is revealed most clearly in the person and work of Christ, but it is not mediated *only* through Christ. Scriptural evidence for this theocentric position would be found in the first Letter of John 4:7–10, as well as in Pauline texts where Christ belongs to God (1 Cor 3:23) and God is the head of Christ (1 Cor 11:3). Finally, in Romans 8:39 Paul speaks powerfully of the love of God *made visible* in Christ Jesus our Lord.

The basis for saying that Jesus is the normative mediator of salvation can come from two directions. First, some hold that this is what Scripture clearly teaches, speaking of Jesus as the Word of God, and God speaking to us in His Son in the fulness of times (Heb 1). Others, Troeltsch for example, conclude to the normativeness of Jesus Christ and Christianity through comparison with other religions.[27] The varied claims are examined in dialogue; then, based upon a view of who man is and who God is, we judge that Jesus Christ is the normative revelation and exemplification of the nature of God and man. Troeltsch writes:

Accordingly, he will be a Christian because he discerns in Christianity the purest and most forceful revelation of the higher world. He will see in the Christian faith not the absolute but the normative religion, the religion that is normative not only for him personally but also for all history up to the present time.[28]

Because this third position on the spectrum is controversial and a genuine *quaestio disputata*, I will refer to several theologians in whose writings we find descriptions of this position. Schubert Ogden, reflecting on the theology of F. D. Maurice, writes that today we need a new reformation in Christian theology: "Whatever else our age may still be willing to accept from us, surely it will no longer hear of a Christianity

---

[27] See Troeltsch's *The Absoluteness of Christianity and the History of Religions* (Richmond, 1971).

[28] *Ibid.*, p. 121.

that is little more than a tribal religion with universal pretensions."[29] He develops this:

> One is still free to affirm that the incarnation of God in Jesus Christ, as real and necessary as it certainly is, does not constitute our human rights and responsibilities, but rather vindicates them . . . . In the same way, one may affirm the necessity of Jesus' sacrificial life and death without in the least supposing that his sacrifice accomplishes some other end than perfectly manifesting God's everlasting purpose to embrace even our sin within his love.[30]

In this interpretation of the Christ event, Jesus is not constitutive of man's salvation but represents and reveals decisively and normatively the universal love of God. The absence of the Christ event would not imply or result in the absence of grace, but rather the absence of the decisive manifestation of grace.

Eugene TeSelle likewise affirms the centrality of Jesus, but speaks against his uniqueness:

> The humanity of Jesus, although it is shaped by and attests to the Word, neither exhausts the Word nor is the sole means of access to it, for the Word is both knowable and efficacious elsewhere. The uniqueness of Jesus—a uniqueness which should not be seen apart from the uniqueness of Israel and the Church—will consist then in being the touchstone by which other responses are judged, the achievement by which their deficiencies are overcome, the center of gravity around which they cluster.[31]

In a criticism of Rahner's doctrine of the anonymous Christian (the second position on our spectrum), TeSelle writes:

> The consequences of his theory of the omnipresence of grace, taken to their full extent, are precisely the opposite of what Rahner himself suggests: it is not that everything must be organized around the one figure of Jesus, but that Jesus is the complete and definitive expression of a relationship between God and man which is present, at least in potentiality, from the very first and which can be acknowledged and approximated to some degree at any time and place.[32]

There is another manner in which this third position might be affirmed. Without explicitly denying that Christ is the constitutive mediator of all salvation, one could hold a sceptical attitude and say we have no evidence to affirm that Jesus Christ is the constitutive mediator for all mankind. Such seems to be the position of H. Richard Niebuhr:

---

[29] Schubert Ogden, "The Reformation That We Want," *Anglican Theological Review* 54 (1972) 268. See also his *Christ without Myth* (New York, 1961) esp. chap. 4.

[30] *Art. cit.*, p. 267 f.

[31] Eugene TeSelle, *Christ in Context* (Philadelphia, 1975) p. 164.

[32] *Ibid.*, p. 163.

So far as I could see and can now see, that miracle has been wrought among us by and through Jesus Christ. I do not have the evidence which allows me to say that the miracle of faith in God is worked only by Jesus Christ and that it is never given to men outside the sphere of his working, though I may say that where I note its presence I posit the presence also of something like Jesus Christ.[33]

Paul Tillich seems to summarize succinctly the third position when he writes: "If he is accepted as the Savior, what does salvation through him mean? The answer cannot be that there is no saving power apart from him, but that he is the ultimate criterion of every healing and saving process . . . . Therefore, wherever there is saving power in mankind, it must be judged by the saving power in Jesus as the Christ."[34]

Ecclesiology

The ecclesiology of this third position is similar to the second ecclesiological stance of the second position, where the Church is a sign of salvation but certainly not its indispensable mediator. Insofar as Christ is normative, the Church can be considered the normative way of salvation. In God's plan the Church is intended to be the community in which the truest and fullest revelation of His love is manifest. The Church is the measure by which other religious communities are judged. But insofar as Jesus Christ himself in this third position is not constitutive, much less can the Church be considered to be the constitutive mediator of salvation.

There seems, however, to be a difference in the attitude of the believer to Jesus in this third position compared with the second. Since it is a more theocentric position, and since Jesus is viewed as the normative but not constitutive mediator of salvation, he is viewed less as the object of faith and more as a model of faith. Jesus Christ points the believer to the Father rather than to himself. In the second position, in contrast, Jesus is viewed as the sole embodiment and realization of God's love, and he is clearly the object of worship. His humanity is holy, seemingly independent of his decisions and actions.[35]

THEOCENTRIC UNIVERSE, NONNORMATIVE CHRISTOLOGY

The third position affirms Jesus Christ as the normative mediator of salvation. In the fourth position, a more sceptical epistemology is operative, maintaining that it is impossible or unnecessary to judge

---

[33] H. Richard Niebuhr, "Reformation: Continuing Imperative," *Christian Century* 77 (1960) 249.

[34] Paul Tillich, *Systematic Theology* 2 (Chicago, 1957) pp. 167–68.

[35] The subsequent essays on the Church by Haight and Sears will present examples of these two different attitudes towards the person of Jesus Christ.

among religions and savior figures. Judgments about claims to uniqueness or normativeness are unverifiable and without basis. Adherents of
this position refuse to make judgments or comparisons about various
religions, and prefer an epistemological relativism or scepticism. This
position could be viewed simply as a negative refusal, but it must also be
viewed in a positive manner insofar as the adherent stresses even more
than the previous position the incomprehensibility of God and the
mystery of human subjectivity. It prefers to let God be God; it cautions
against making God and His ways into our image, and against trying to
judge Him and His ways by our human standards. Its posture is that of
Job when he exclaims in reverent awe before the mystery of God: "I have
been holding forth on matters I cannot understand, on marvels beyond
me and my knowledge" (Jb 42:3). It echoes the mysterious ways of God
to which Jesus refers when he boldly asserts that "men from east and
west, from north and south, will come to take their places at the feast in
the kingdom of God" (Lk 13:29).

In this position, therefore, there are many mediators of salvation and
Jesus Christ is one of them. To move from this neutralist position to one
which affirms that Jesus is either normative or constitutive is to move
beyond the evidence at hand. Perhaps a person like Thomas Jefferson
exemplifies this model in his writings.[36] He writes of the advantages and
disadvantages of the system of morals which Jesus presented, and
concludes that they could be considered the most perfect and sublime
ever taught by man. Jesus is the great teacher or enlightener, leading his
followers in the search for wisdom. In a similar manner, Ralph Waldo
Emerson speaks critically of the Christian Churches, although he does
look favorably upon Jesus as belonging to the true race of prophets.
Jesus, according to Emerson, can be considered a true mediator in that
sense only in which possibly any being can mediate between God and
man—that is, an instructor of man. He teaches us how to become like
God.[37]

There can be an intense loyalty to Jesus Christ and his cause, but it is
not such that we make the further step of placing him in a unique or even
normative position in regard to other great figures of history and other
ways of salvation. The ecclesiological position clearly follows. There are
many communities of salvation, for God has no special, favored way in
which we are to achieve salvation.

Is this fourth position a legitimate and tenable Christian position? In

[36] Among the varied writings of Jefferson, see his *Life and Morals of Jesus of Nazareth,
Extracted Textually from the Gospels.*

[37] A key essay of Emerson that manifests this position is his famous "Divinity School
Address."

the Roman Catholic Church's reaction to certain movements of the nineteenth century, it is clearly disallowed. For example, in Pius IX's *Syllabus of Errors* (1864), theses 15 to 18 of Section 3 are specifically directed against attitudes of religious indifferentism or latitudinarianism, which would assert that all religions are equal. Yet, when the fourth position is viewed positively in its emphasis upon the incomprehensibility of God and acknowledges Jesus as a way of salvation for his followers, it seems to be more viable and not merely a negative position of religious laxity or indifferentism.

Paul Tillich, for example, refers to the mystical critical element in human existence. We come to see that all our formulations about God are inadequate and that we must somehow go beyond them. While it is true that we do need embodiments of the Ultimate, these are secondary.[38] So, too, Rahner indicates in several of his essays that God is always found as mystery, as the incomprehensible one.[39] Even God's revelation of Himself in Jesus does not remove the mystery; in fact, as with all knowledge, according to Rahner, it makes it more of a mystery. Thus the revelation of God in Christ could be considered as deepening rather than lessening the mystery of God's salvific ways for mankind. While the conviction that God is love grows deeper, the question of how God's salvific love illuminates mankind can become ever more mysterious. Rahner has called the Christian the true and most radical sceptic. He can hold no opinion to be completely true and no opinion to be completely false.[40] I suggest these thoughts from Tillich and Rahner to remind the theologian of the caution with which he makes his theological statements. Elements of this theological caution lead persons to move to this fourth and most tolerant position on the spectrum.

In addition to the more directly theological rationale based upon the incomprehensibility of God, a reason that might lead to this position is a careful observation of the actual history of religions. Such is the case with Arnold Toynbee. He would argue that the study of the history of religions reveals no movement of religions towards Christianity or Jesus Christ as unique or even normative. The more we examine particular religious traditions, the more we are struck by their individual characteristics and differing viewpoints. Thus it becomes more difficult to make judgments

---

[38] Paul Tillich, "The Significance of the History of Religions for the Systematic Theologian," in *The Future of Religions*, ed. Jerald Brauer (New York, 1966) p. 87. See also Tillich's concluding section in his *The Courage to Be* (New Haven, 1952) for his thoughts on the God above God.

[39] See, e.g., his essay on "Mystery" in *Sacramentum mundi* 4. This point of view is powerfully expressed in the address Rahner delivered at the University of Chicago, Nov. 5, 1975, on "Thomas Aquinas on the Incomprehensibility of God."

[40] The final pages of the talk referred to above (n. 39) express this viewpoint.

of uniqueness or normativeness among religions, for these judgments all too often are unfair or inadequate to the richness and complexity of the particular religions.

We ought also, I should say, to try to purge our Christianity of the traditional Christian belief that Christianity is unique. This is not just a Western Christian belief: it is intrinsic to Christianity itself. All the same, I suggest that we have to do this if we are to purge Christianity of the exclusive-mindedness and intolerance that follows from a belief in Christianity's uniqueness.[41]

FURTHER IMPLICATIONS

If the spectrum of four views I have presented is clarifying in terms of Christology and ecclesiology, then it should also be of assistance in clarifying positions in related areas of Christian theology. Instead of developing these areas at length, I present them in the form of a diagram (Figure II).

I set this forth again with the caution that I am making generalizations and that at times the pieces do not fit. But I do it with the conviction that the spectrum does exemplify larger viewpoints, attitudes, and methodological differences that are significant in Christian theology today. To expand on this, I will lift from the diagram several suggestive lines of inquiry in the area of method and basic viewpoints that seem to be exemplified by the four positions of the spectrum. Three areas to be briefly examined are (1) the attitude to the non-Christian world as the dialogical partner of theology, (2) the attitude to specifically Christian sources and resources, and (3) indications of theological method involved in the four positions.

1) *Attitude to the non-Christian world as a dialogical partner in theology.* The first position (ecclesiocentric) looks with total negativeness upon the non-Christian world, as the place of error. There is no purpose in a two-way dialogue; there is only a call to conversion. The second position, anonymous Christianity, views the non-Christian world as ordered to Christ, with its truth and good ultimately derived from and indeed constituted by Christ. It engages in dialogue but ultimately interprets the non-Christian world in terms of Christian categories. Thus it is relatively open-minded. The third position, theocentric, is more open and positive towards non-Christian realities, since it sees the non-Christian world as a place of genuine revelation and as a way to God. It can learn from non-Christians about the same God whom it sees normatively revealed in Christ, for all religions are mediations of divine

---

[41] This quotation from Toynbee is from his key essay "What Should Be the Christian Approach to the Contemporary Non-Christian Faiths?" in *Attitudes toward Other Religions*, ed. Owen Thomas (London, 1969) pp. 160–61.

FIGURE II

Topic area	1) Jesus Christ exclusive mediator	2) Jesus Christ constitutive mediator	3) Jesus Christ normative mediator	4) Jesus Christ one of many mediators
Extent of God's saving grace and love	limited to Christians	through Christ to all	to all, and manifest most clearly in Christ	to all in different ways
Kingdom of God and Spirit of God	identified with the Church	present only through Christ, for all	manifest most fully in Christ, for all	available for all
Attitude of Christian to non-Christian world	negative attitude, since it is place of sin and error	receptive to action of God in the world interpreted Christologically	receptive, open, maintaining Christ as norm of God's activity	positive attitude, with God operative universally
Attitude to other religions	other religions as absolutely false	other religions as relatively false, pre-Christian	others as relatively true, yet normed by Jesus Christ	true, valid ways of salvation
Christian missionary attitudes	bring all into the Church	point all to Christ so as to make explicit what is already implicit	point to Christ as normative way, and learn from dialogue	dialogue, but allow diversity of religion
The individual is saved by	orthodoxy necessary	orthodoxy and orthopraxis	orthopraxis as primary	orthopraxis as sole criterion
Sinfulness is overcome by	strong sense of sin, overcome by Christ in his Church	Christ as the exclusive way beyond sin	Christ as the normative way beyond sin	many ways to overcome sin
Type of Christology	high Christology, Trinity and hypostatic union	high Christology, Trinity and hypostatic union	low Christology, stress the humanity of Jesus	low Christology
Christ event is salvific by	ontological power of the Incarnation of Christ efficient causality	ontological power of the life, death, resurrection of Christ efficient causality primarily	moral power of the teaching, life, death, resurrection of Christ exemplary causality primarily	moral power of the teaching, life, death, resurrection of Christ exemplary causality

salvific truth. The fourth position, the extreme opposite of the first, refuses from epistemological grounds to make judgments among religions. In dialogue it must accept the given pluralism, since it sees no way to move beyond pluralism to make judgments of normativeness. Thus, in the final analysis, it is a passive partner in dialogue between religions.

2) *Attitude to specifically Christian sources and resources.* In the first position, Scripture and Christian dogma are the final and absolute criteria for truth, unassailable by non-Christian viewpoints or even by contemporary experience. The Scriptures, which are often read in an inadequate proof-text manner, are normative over contemporary experience. In the second position, Scripture and tradition retain their normativeness but are examined more critically and historically. They are interpreted in terms of their response to their situation and not in a fundamentalistic sense made applicable to all times and places. Thus adequacy for contemporary experience becomes a norm or guideline, in addition to Scripture and tradition. In the third position, Scripture and tradition are viewed as normative for the believer but not for nonbelievers. Other religious sources and traditions function salvifically for other religions, even though in dialogue we would maintain that we can point to the superiority or normativeness of the Christian witness. This conviction of the normativeness of Christianity is not imposed upon other religions, nor even used to interpret other religions from our Christian perspective. In the fourth position, Scripture and tradition remain an important way for the Christian but are surely not the only way to discover God. The epistemological attitude of this position denies that we can adequately understand other religious traditions to which we do not belong, so as to make comparisons between Christian and non-Christian sources and resources.

3) *Indications of theological method involved in the four positions.* In the first position, theology proceeds from above, from religious documents that are norms above space and time. It is highly dogmatic and universalistic in its attitude, with little or no attempt at a correlation of Christian sources and contemporary questions and experiences. In the second position, correlation takes place, but from the conviction of the ultimate truth of the Christian witness. Thus it, too, is basically dogmatic and universalistic, although it is more open to, and involved in, concrete historical experience. It seems to rely upon a universal ontology in its affirmations concerning the constitutive function of Jesus Christ. The third position moves from a universalist and dogmatic towards a historical and existential viewpoint. Individuals and groups in dialogue with other individuals and groups become the locus for truth and intelligibility. Jesus Christ emerges as normative from below, from historical experience. Thus, while this position may contain elements of

an ontology or may find itself moving towards an ontology, that ontology will be formed from below, with its ultimate intelligibility emerging from history. In the fourth position, the shift continues, from dogmatism through universalism through historical intelligibility, to focus upon epistemological problems. It affirms that there is no point from which we can affirm that Jesus Christ is the constitutive or even normative way of salvation.

CONCLUDING SUMMARY

I conclude with a brief evaluative statement of each of the four positions. The first position, exclusive ecclesiocentricism, seems clearly out of touch with our common experience of the values and spiritual resources of non-Christian religions. It is unacceptable because of its closed nature, its refusal to join in discussion with opposing viewpoints.

The second position, an inclusive, constitutive Christology, does take into account the values of non-Christian realities, even though in the final analysis it interprets them from the Christian perspective. It does seem to be the mainline Christian position, exemplified, for example, in Catholicism in Vatican II. But it seems that it will continually be under attack from a more liberal position, based either upon the manner in which it selects from and interprets the Scriptures, or upon the more general and encompassing question of the historical nature of all human understanding.

The third position, theocentric, with a normative Christology, can join more readily in dialogue with non-Christian religions and affirm its theistic position. The dialogue of differences resides on the level of mediations rather than ultimates and ends. The advantage of this position is its openness to dialogue and its high respect for other religious traditions. Two questions may be put to it. First, in affirming Jesus Christ as normative, does it not find itself moving in the direction of the previous position, and asking what is the basis of this normativeness? Secondly, from the other direction, does it not have to respond to the challenge of epistemology and establish more critically how it can affirm that Jesus Christ is superior or normative in relation to other savior figures?

The fourth position, where Jesus is one of many mediators, seems somewhat ineffective in an age of pluralism, since it affirms that we cannot make decisions among religions and religious savior figures. It is an attractive position because of its cautious scepticism, because of its tolerance of other positions, and because of its emphasis upon the majesty and mystery of the divine.

As I have indicated, it would seem that the most important discussion among Christian theologians is between those who affirm the second or the third positions. Both positions demand that we take Christ and culture, the Church and the world, with utter seriousness. Neither of the two poles can be dissolved, minimalized, or left out of the discussion. In the first position, the pole of the world and culture is definitely left out; in the fourth position, the pole of Christ and Church, as traditionally understood by Christian theology, is minimalized.

Obviously, discussion on the merits of the various positions could continue. But the major thrust of this essay is to serve as an introduction, to lead into the following related essays, which focus upon ecclesiology in the Scriptures, in tradition, and in contemporary theology. If this essay is successful in setting forth a spectrum of positions and categories in Christology and ecclesiology that will be of assistance in subsequent discussions, it will have achieved its main purpose.

II

NEW TESTAMENT COMMUNITIES IN TRANSITION: A STUDY OF MATTHEW AND LUKE

EUGENE A. LaVERDIERE, S.S.S., and
WILLIAM G. THOMPSON, S.J.*

Jesuit School of Theology in Chicago

THE RECOGNITION of biblical theology as a separate and autonomous discipline has challenged the Church to rethink how it uses Scripture in its practice of prayer, in its preaching, in its liturgical life, and in its theology. The process toward this recognition began in the Roman Catholic Church when biblical criticism was reintroduced by Pius XII. Biblical studies have since then gradually, if sometimes reluctantly, been accepted into the mainstream of Catholic thought. Such acceptance has, however, brought us to what Raymond E. Brown has described as "the current painful assimilation of the implications of biblical criticism for Catholic doctrine, theology, and practice."[1] This article is intended to contribute to that assimilation by presenting data from the writings of Matthew and Luke judged relevant to the question "Why the Church?"

Biblical theology is a historical discipline. Its first and most crucial task is to provide an empathetic description and understanding of the biblical writings, each on its own terms. It uses categories appropriate to the culture in which these writings emerged. It interprets what they meant in their historical setting without borrowing categories from later times. It provides, in Krister Stendahl's terms, "a frontal nonpragmatic, nonapologetic attempt to describe OT or NT faith and practice from within its own presuppositions, and with due attention to its own organizing principles, regardless of its possible ramifications for those who live by the Bible as the Word of God."[2] The primary task in this article, then, is to describe how Matthew and Luke thought about the role and function of the Church, each in his own historical context.

The descriptive task alone, however, does not show how these writings can inspire Christian theology today, or how they are to be accepted by contemporary theologians as a *norma normans non normata*. Such questions are important for theologians who believe that Matthew and Luke not only had a meaning in the past but also have a meaning in the

---

* EDITOR'S NOTE—W. G. Thompson has written the introduction, the section on Matthew, and the conclusion; E. A. LaVerdiere has written the section on Luke.

[1] *The Virginal Conception and Bodily Resurrection of Jesus* (New York, 1973) p. 3. For a statement of the biblical suppositions for this article, see pp. 15–20; also R. E. Brown, K. P. Donfried, J. Reumann, eds., *Peter in the New Testament* (New York, 1973) pp. 7–22.

[2] "Biblical Theology, Contemporary," in *The Interpreter's Dictionary of the Bible* 1 (New York, 1962) 425.

present. They are answered within the consciousness of the Church, a consciousness that accepts New Testament writings as sacred and canonical, expecting them somehow to inform and influence the Church's ongoing life and theology. Consequently, once we have described how Matthew and Luke thought about the Church, we will offer tentative suggestions as to how their writings might inspire theologians and function as normative in their thinking about the Church today.

To discover how Matthew and Luke can inform and influence contemporary understandings of the Church, we must first recognize that the context of their questions was not the same as ours, that their world view was significantly different from ours. They explained the *raison d'être* of local communities. Communication among them had just begun to be established. Matthew's largely Jewish-Christian community had little or no contact with or influence on the predominantly Gentile-Christian communities addressed by Luke. The Evangelists also thought these local communities would continue to exist only until the second coming of Jesus Christ. Whatever ties they established with Judaism, with Hellenistic culture, and with the Roman Empire would be temporary, passing away at the Parousia. Furthermore, since Matthew and Luke imagined the world to be limited to the Roman Empire, they may well have expected that the gospel could be preached to the whole world in a short time. The Church's mission was clearly universal not only in intention but also with the hope of actual fulfilment. Finally, Matthew and Luke expressed their understanding of the Church's function in stories about Jesus and the early Church. Matthew narrated the life of Jesus from his conception to his resurrection, guided by a historical perspective that would enable his readers to find their own experience reflected in the narrative. Luke introduced "history" as a literary form, so that his second-generation Gentile communities could see precisely how they remained in continuity with Jesus of Nazareth and his immediate followers.

Our situation is very different. We ask about the role and function of the universal Church, a Church that spans the entire world and speaks to that world through an efficient network of communication. The result is that our thinking about the Church must take into account the vast cultural pluralism that exists today. We are also aware that, as a long-established institution, the universal Church has a complex social, economic, and political history. It has established and maintained multiple relations to secular institutions at the local, national, and international levels. It cannot put them aside or exist without them. We recognize, furthermore, that the world population is so vast that we cannot expect to announce the gospel to even a significant number of the men and women alive today. Our thinking about the Church's mission must be very different from that of Matthew and Luke. Finally, theologians today do more than retell stories about Jesus and the early Church. We speak several languages at once: the descriptive language of the Gospel narratives, the propositional language of creedal formulae and doctrinal statements, and the technical language of systematic theology. The distance, then, that separates Matthew and Luke from later creeds and dogmas, from the institutional Church, and from our modern situation makes us realize that they thought about the Church in a context very different from our own. A creative tension must be maintained between these two situations.[3]

Despite the distance, however, theologians in every age claim that the biblical writings, such as Matthew and Luke, constitute the norm, the *norma normans non normata*, for Christian theology. For some the Bible functions as a negative norm. They seek to understand the Church from the data of contemporary experience, formulate their understanding in nonbiblical language, and then ask whether it is consistent with the Bible. For other theologians, however, the Bible also has a more positive function. They develop an understanding of the Church both from contemporary experience and from the Bible. The biblical writings inform, influence, and positively inspire them in their search for understanding.[4] Neither group of theologians affirms that because the Bible is the Word of God, it must speak the same literal message to every age. Nor do they consider the biblical writings so culturally conditioned that they cannot speak to our present situation. Both groups agree that the Bible is the norm for Christian theology, but they disagree on the way it functions as norm.[5]

Another way to describe how the Bible can function as a positive norm in theology is to say that it provides contemporary theologians with "paradigms" that inform, influence, and inspire them as they think about the Church. James M. Gustafson has provided a useful description of biblical paradigms:

[3] *Ibid.*, pp. 425–30. For further discussion see W. Wink, *The Bible in Human Transformation: Toward a New Paradigm for Biblical Study* (Philadelphia, 1973) pp. 19–31; R. E. Brown, "The Current Crisis in Theology as It Affects the Teaching of Catholic Doctrine," in his *Biblical Reflections on Crises Facing the Church* (New York, 1975) pp. 3–19.

[4] Both Roger Haight and Robert Sears, later in this issue, use Scripture as a positive norm, but they differ in the extent to which they allow the Bible to influence their understanding of the Church. Haight bases his understanding on the biblical symbol "mission"; Sears builds his understanding of the Church as community on data from both the Old and the New Testaments.

[5] For the spectrum of different uses of Scripture, see J. Peter Schineller's article in this issue.

Paradigms are basic models of a vision of life, and of the practice of life, from which flow certain consistent attitudes, outlooks (or "onlooks"), rules or norms of behavior, and specific actions. . . . Rather the paradigm *in*-forms and *in*-fluences the life of the community and its members as they become what they are under their own circumstances. By *in*-form I wish to suggest more than giving data or information; I wish to suggest a formation of life. By *in*-fluence I wish to suggest a flowing into the life of the community and its members. A paradigm allows for the community and its members to make it their own, to bring it into the texture and fabric of life that exists, conditioned as that is by its historical circumstances, by the sorts of limitations and extensions of particular capacities and powers that exist in persons and communities.[6]

As paradigms, the Matthean and Lukan writings can inform and influence the Church in its prayer life, in its preaching, in its liturgical life, or in its theology. In this article we limit our reflections to how they can influence contemporary theology.

One can begin to determine a biblical paradigm either from the texture and fabric of life in the Church today or from the biblical writings themselves. In this series of articles we are beginning from the contemporary experience of radical change, the type of change that leads to a new self-understanding and calls for new patterns of behavior. Events that have shaped our understanding of "the modern world"—wars, technology, industrialism, communications media, Darwin, Freud, Marx, Nietzsche, Kierkegaard, etc.—have also caused the Church to question her behavior and identity. Such a change is perhaps best illustrated in Roman Catholicism. Langdon Gilkey has described the scene from a Protestant perspective:

> To those both within and without her massive walls, present-day Roman Catholicism presents a scene of vast, almost unrelieved confusion. . . . Many of her fundamental practices have slipped away; her most cherished dogmas and sacrosanct authorities are scorned by many and ignored or questioned by most; her formerly changeless patterns of life are altered by an accelerating flux of fads; and her treasured unity is broken by intense inner conflicts.[7]

Matthew and Luke have been selected from the New Testament precisely because these Evangelists wrote for communities in transition.[8] Matthew's largely Jewish-Christian community had come to see themselves no longer as a sectarian group within Judaism but as an

---

[6] "The Relation of the Gospels to the Moral Life," in D. G. Miller and D. Y. Hadidian, eds., *Jesus and Man's Hope* 2 (Pittsburgh, 1971) 111.

[7] *Catholicism Confronts Modernity: A Protestant View* (New York, 1975) p. 2.

[8] The choice of Matthew and Luke, rather than Paul and John, may surprise theologians unfamiliar with redaction-critical and composition-critical studies of the New Testament, which stress the role of the Synoptic Evangelists as theologians. See N. Perrin, *What Is Redaction Criticism?* (Philadelphia, 1969).

independent religious movement founded by Jesus, the Jewish Messiah. The Lukan communities, predominantly Gentile-Christians, faced the challenge of integrating their Hellenistic culture and their existence in the Roman political world with their conversion to Christianity, a religion founded by a Jew from Nazareth. Both Evangelists presented their communities with a new understanding of what it meant to be Christians and how they should live in their contemporary world.

In this article, then, we are principally concerned to describe how Matthew and Luke thought about the Church in a time of transition. We will conclude, however, with suggestions about how their understandings might function as normative for Christian theologians as they attempt to understand the Church today. Our suggestions will remain tentative, since biblical theologians can decide what is normative only in dialogue with the entire theological community within the Church.

MATTHEW

The concrete situation, addressed by Matthew in his Gospel, can be described as follows. First, Matthew wrote for a group of predominantly but not exclusively Jewish-Christians. Secondly, his work can be dated about fifteen years after the Jewish war which ended with the destruction of Jerusalem and the Temple, that is, around A.D. 85. Thirdly, he and his community were situated in a place, most likely Palestine or Syria, where recent developments within Judaism, especially the growth of Jamnia Pharisaism, largely determined the religious environment. Finally, the Evangelist faced confusion, tension, conflict, and the destructive influence of false prophets within the community. To substantiate these statements, we must look at the Gospel itself. How does it mirror and hence reveal this situation?[9]

Matthean scholars broadly agree that the Christians in Matthew's community were largely, but not exclusively, converts from Judaism. They argue from the obvious "Jewishness" of the first Gospel. The Matthean Jesus is the Messiah, the Son of David, promised in the Old Testament and eagerly awaited by the Jews.[10] Furthermore, Matthew rooted Jesus' origin and his ministry of teaching, preaching, and healing in the Jewish past through several explicit quotations of the Old Testament and even more indirect allusions.[11] He is also more concerned than the other Evangelists with the Christian attitude toward the

[9] For an excellent summary of recent work on Matthew, see D. J. Harrington, "Matthean Studies since Joachim Rohde," *Heythrop Journal* 16 (1975) 375-88.

[10] Mt 1:1-17; 9:27; 12:22-24; 15:22; 20:30-31; 21:9; 21:14-17; 22:41-46.

[11] The so-called "formula quotations" (Mt 1:22-23; 2:5-6; 2:15; 2:17-18; 2:23b; 4:14-16; 8:17; 12:18-21; 13:35; 21:4-5; 27:9-10) have long been recognized as a distinctive Matthean characteristic. For recent discussion see Harrington, *art. cit.*, pp. 386-87.

religious institutions of Judaism, especially the law and the cult.[12] Consequently, the Christians for whom Matthew wrote his Gospel must have had the religious and cultural background necessary to understand his portrayal of Jesus and the disciples. They must have, for example, been familiar with the Old Testament and the practices of Jewish piety. In a word, they must have been to a large extent converts from Judaism.

W. D. Davies has called attention to the fact that even though the Jewish war (A.D. 66–70) and the destruction of Jerusalem and the Temple (A.D. 70) did not profoundly influence the over-all development of Christianity, these events did in fact have a profound impact on Matthew and his community. Davies has summarized the direct evidence as follows:

In two passages, he [Matthew] introduces what can hardly be other than direct references to these [events]. In the parable of the wedding feast, in xxii. 1 ff., the anger of the king with the recalcitrant elect, that is, the Jews, is expressed in what is almost certainly a reference to the siege and fall of the city. "The King was angry, and he sent his troops and destroyed those murderers and burned their city" (xxii. 7). That is, the rejection of Israel is discussed particularly in connexion with A.D. 70. Equally significant, and consonant with this, is that Matthew places the poignant cry of Jesus over Jerusalem at the close of his anti-Pharisaic discourse. The culmination of that indictment and its vindication he states in xxiii. 37f.: "O Jerusalem, Jerusalem. . . . Behold, your house [temple] is forsaken and desolate" (RSV). . . . It is followed immediately in chapter xxiv by the discussion of the Parousia, which in Matthew has been interpreted by Feuillet as the divine judgment on Judaism in the fall of Jerusalem and which, in any case, includes that event (xxiv. 1–3).[13]

Other minor indications also reveal Matthew's concern with the city of Jerusalem: the reference to Jerusalem in the first Passion-prediction (16:21), the disturbance of the whole city at Jesus' entrance (21:10–11). At his death those raised from the dead "went into the holy city" (27:53), and after his resurrection the custodians at the tomb "went into the city" to report what had happened (28:11). This data suggests that we date the final composition of the Gospel at a time when the events of the Jewish war, especially the destruction of Jersusalem and the Temple, had already caused Matthew's largely Jewish-Christian community to reflect on their identity, that is, around A.D. 85.

It has also been widely recognized since Davies' work that central to the Matthean community's struggle to understand themselves as Christians in a changing world was the question of how they should relate to recent developments within Judaism, especially the emergence of

---

[12] See Harrington, art. cit., pp. 380–81, 387.

[13] The Setting of the Sermon on the Mount (Cambridge, Eng., 1964) pp. 298–99.

Jamnia Pharisaism. The Pharisees at Jamnia, with Johannan ben Zakkai their leader, were assuming exclusive power. They saw to it that their only remaining rivals, the Sadducees, were discredited, and they found ways to contain the traditionally powerful priesthood. Johannan gained control of the calendar, indicating by this act that the Beth Din at Jamnia had taken over an important function of the Great Sanhedrin in Jerusalem. Control of the calendar was crucial for a religion based on the observance of the law. Johannan also assumed the right to regulate the conduct of priests in worship. He transferred to the synagogues a part of the Temple ritual, and he legislated about the gifts and offerings normally due to the Temple. Within Pharisaism the conflicts between the Hillelites and the Shammaites were gradually resolved in favor of the former, and codification was introduced into the previously chaotic interpretation of the law. Also in the interests of unification, the sages at Jamnia attempted to regulate the synagogue worship. To awaken popular sentiment, they linked its service to that of the now defunct Temple. But at the same time they standardized the traditional service, concentrated on the problem of the canon of Scripture, and instituted the rabbinate as the authoritative interpreter of the law. Finally, Jamnian Judaism consciously confronted Christianity. The Birkath ha Minim, the use of the ban, and other tendencies, both liturgical and nonliturgical, were introduced to deal with the rising significance of this new religious sect.[14]

Such dramatic changes in Judaism profoundly disturbed the Matthean community. Their self-understanding had been rooted in Jewish tradition. But as Jamnia Pharisaism rose to prominence, they were forced to question their relation to Judaism and even their own identity. Could they continue as a sect within Judaism? Should they accept or reject the self-understanding promoted by the sages? Were they to continue their mission to the Jews? What attitude should they take toward the law? Matthew wrote his Gospel in large part to awaken a new self-understanding in the light of these circumstances. He wrote in dialogue with the recent developments at Jamnia, to show his community what it meant to be Christians in the changing milieu of postwar Judaism.

Within the community confusion and doubt prevailed; for what the Matthean Jesus predicts as future events describes the present experience of Matthew's community: "Then they will deliver you up to tribulation, and put you to death; and you will be hated by all nations for my name's sake. And then many will fall away, and betray one another, and hate one another. And many false prophets will arise and lead many

[14] For a full treatment of these developments at Jamnia, see Davies, *ibid.*, pp. 256–86.

astray. And because wickedness is multiplied, most men's love will grow cold. But he who endures to the end will be saved" (24:9–13).[15] Matthew and his community, then, had to confront important issues: persecution from non-Jewish sources, scandal caused by mutual betrayal, hatred between members, the divisive influence of false prophets, and widespread wickedness causing love itself to grow cold.

In dialogue with Jamnia Pharisaism and in response to these tensions within his community, Matthew retold the story of Jesus from his conception to after his resurrection. The author of Luke–Acts, as we shall see, chose to tell both the story of Jesus (Lk) and the story of the early Christian community (Acts). But Matthew so selected, arranged, and composed his material that his readers might find themselves in the narrative. He created a distinctive portrait of Jesus, his followers, and his opponents. Members of his community could identify with the disciples and see the opponents as surrogates for the sages at Jamnia. Matthew could address them through the words and actions of Jesus.[16]

Matthew stressed four themes. First, and above all, he presented his community with a new understanding of their mission. They had been sent to "the lost sheep of the house of Israel." But now they should devote themselves to the wider Gentile mission. Secondly, to carry out that mission, he urged them no longer to understand themselves as a sectarian group within Judaism. Recent developments indicated that they should accept their separation from Jamnia Pharisaism and claim an independent identity with roots in Jesus Christ and the Jewish Messiahs and through him in their Jewish past. Thirdly, Matthew urged reconciliation, forgiveness, and mutual love within the community; for the Gentile mission would never succeed unless the community learned how to manage the confusion, tension, and conflict that divided them one from another. Finally, as motivation for the Gentile mission, Matthew assured his community that when the Son of Man comes, he will judge not only themselves but also the Gentiles to whom they are sent. We shall describe each theme in greater detail.

Gentile Mission

Exegetes have long recognized that the final commission "to make disciples of all Gentiles" (28:16–20) dominates Matthew's historical and

---

[15] For a full exposition of this passage, cf. W. G. Thompson, "An Historical Perspective in the Gospel of Matthew," *Journal of Biblical Literature* 93 (1974) 243–62.

[16] An approach to the Gospels as "dramatic history" has been suggested by R. M. Frye, "A Literary Perspective for the Criticism of the Gospels," in *Jesus and Man's Hope* (n. 6 above) 2, 193–221. I understand the Matthean narrative as comparable to a drama on-stage. The action is the narrative itself, the Evangelist is the playwright-director off-stage, and the community is the audience. Matthew speaks to his community, like the playwright-director, through the action in the narrative. His message and their situation can be discovered principally by looking at the action on-stage.

theological perspective.[17] It is the one event that must be completed before the end can come: "And this gospel of the kingdom will be preached throughout the whole world, as a testimony to all Gentiles; and then the end will come" (24:14). And the commission is given in an appearance of the risen Lord for which the Matthean Jesus has carefully prepared his followers; for at the Last Supper Jesus announces that, once risen from the dead, he will go before his disciples into Galilee (26:31–32). And both the angel and the risen Jesus tell the women at the empty tomb to carry this message to his disciples: "he is going before you to Galilee; there you will see him" (28:7, 10).

The commission itself is simple and unadorned. Jesus appears to his disciples, and they see him. Some worship him, but others doubt. Jesus presents himself as all-powerful, commissions them to make disciples of all Gentiles, and promises his abiding presence to the end (28:18–20).

Studies of this passage have shown that it is best understood as a revelation. Jesus reveals that, as their risen and exalted Lord, he has come into the full possession of all power. That is, the power he formerly exercised in his mission to Israel now extends to all the earth. Such a turning point in Jesus' career also marks a change for the disciples. Their mission had been formerly limited, like Jesus' mission, to "the lost sheep of the house of Israel" (10:5b–6). But now it extends to all the Gentiles. Continuity with the past is assured, since the same disciples are now sent to baptize all Gentiles and to teach everything that Jesus has taught them.

Even though in his earthly life the Matthean Jesus is sent "to the lost sheep of the house of Israel" (15:24), Matthew focuses on Gentiles throughout his Gospel narrative. The Magi, pagan astrologers, come from the East to pay homage to Jesus, precisely as the Messiah of Israel, while in Jerusalem Herod seeks to destroy him (2:1–23). Prior to the cure of his servant, the pagan centurion is commended for his faith, as Jesus tells the crowds: "Truly, I say to you, not even in Israel have I found such faith" (8:10). Similarly, the Canaanite woman models confidence in Jesus' power and willingness to heal her daughter, and is granted her request with these words: "O woman, great is your faith! Be it done for you as you desire" (15:28). In the parable of the wicked husbandman Jesus warns the Jewish religious leaders: "Therefore I tell you, the kingdom of God will be taken from you and given to a nation producing the fruits of it" (21:43). Finally, at the death of Jesus it is the Roman centurion and those with him who profess "Truly this was the Son of God!" (27:54). These episodes reveal the message of Matthew to his community. Throughout the lifetime of Jesus himself non-Jews believed in him.

[17] For discussion and bibliography, see Thompson, art. cit. (n. 15 above) pp. 259–60. Also D. R. A. Hare and D. J. Harrington, "Make Disciples of All the Gentiles (Matthew 28:19)," Catholic Biblical Quarterly 37 (1975) 359 69.

Certainly now, long after his death, his followers should not be afraid to preach the gospel to the Gentiles and welcome them into their community.

It is not surprising, then, that Matthew concluded his narrative with the explicit commission to "make disciples of all Gentiles" (28:19). Matthew emphasized the Gentile mission, so that his largely Jewish-Christian community might understand that in the changing world of postwar Judaism they were sent to preach the gospel to the Gentile world.

Judaism

To support the Gentile mission, Matthew needed to show his community that they were no longer a sectarian group within Judaism but had become an independent movement separate from Jamnia Pharisaism and rooted in Jesus Christ. Matthew communicated this self-understanding by portraying Jesus as the Jewish Messiah, as an authoritative teacher, and as in tension with the scribes and Pharisees.

The Matthean Jesus is the Christ, the Messiah promised in the Old Testament and eagerly awaited by the Jews. Matthew demonstrated this truth in the prologue (1:11-2:23) by providing apologetic and scriptural answers to questions concerning the origin of Jesus and the place of his birth.[18] How can Jesus be the Messiah? In the genealogy Matthew traces his lineage through Joseph to David and Abraham, placing him in the direct line of Jewish history and messianic expectations (1:1-17). He then explains how Jesus' origin and his name were revealed to Joseph (1:18-25). Why, then, does he not come from Bethlehem rather than Nazareth? Matthew resolves this dilemma with a journey from Bethlehem to Egypt and back to Nazareth (2:1-23). Each event in the narrative—the visit of the Magi, the flight into Egypt, the massacre of the innocents, and the return to Nazareth—is presented as the fulfilment of an Old Testament text.[19]

Matthew also uses quotations from the Old Testament to interpret the public ministry of Jesus: his move to Capharnaum, his healings, his use of parables, and his entry into Jerusalem.[20] And the title "Son of David" occurs throughout the Gospel.[21] In this way Matthew does not let the reader forget that Jesus is the Messiah promised in the Old Testament and eagerly awaited by the Jews.

The Matthean Jesus is also an authoritative ethical teacher, certainly

---

[18] See K. Stendahl. "Quis et Unde?: An Analysis of Mt 1-2," in *Judentum-Urchristentum-Kirche* (Berlin, 1964) pp. 94-105.

[19] Mt 2:5-6, 15, 17-18, 23b.

[20] Mt 4:14-16; 8:17; 12:18-21; 13:35; 24:4-5.

[21] Mt 9:27; 12:22-24; 15:22; 21:9; 21:14-17.

a rabbi, perhaps the new Moses.[22] He urges his followers to do the will of his Father in heaven.[23] To reveal that will, Jesus does not abolish the law and the prophets, but rather fulfils them by interpreting six statements of the law according to the more essential command, the love of God and neighbor.[24] He promises a future reward to those who do what he says, and he threatens punishment for those who do not.[25] And after his resurrection he commissions his eleven disciples to teach the Gentiles "to observe all that I have commanded you" (28:20). Matthew presents Jesus as the sole authoritative teacher, so that his community will follow his teaching rather than that of the sages at Jamnia.

Matthew's Jesus also argues with the scribes and Pharisees and teaches about them in parables. In Galilee the Pharisees react with hostility when Jesus cures the sick, and Jesus challenges their reaction.[26] He also argues with them about plucking grain on the Sabbath and about healing on the Sabbath (12:1-8, 9-14). But in the Temple in Jerusalem the debates grow into open conflict. Jesus talks about the Jewish religious establishment in parables concerning two sons and the tenants in the vineyard. The chief priests and Pharisees are aware that he is talking about them and seek to arrest him (21:28-46). But Jesus only teaches more explicitly about them in the parable of the wedding feast (22:1-14). The Pharisees continue to plot against him, send their disciples to question him about paying taxes to Caesar, watch the Sadducees ask about the resurrection, and then challenge him themselves about the great commandment (22:15-40). Jesus then takes the initiative in asking the assembled Pharisees about the Messiah (22:41-45). Matthew then adds the comment "And no one was able to answer him a word, nor from that day did anyone dare to ask him any more questions" (22:46). His readers could easily recognize in the debates between Jesus and the Pharisees their own debates with Jamnia Pharisaism.

The Matthean Jesus also warns his disciples and the crowds about the scribes and Pharisees. In the Sermon on the Mount he tells them that their righteousness must surpass that of the scribes and Pharisees, and later applies that principle to almsgiving, prayer, and fasting.[27] After arguing with the Pharisees about ritual cleanliness, he warns his

---

[22] For discussion of the Moses typology in Matthew, see Davies, *op. cit.* (n. 13 above) pp. 25-108.

[23] Mt 6:10; 7:21; 12:46-50; 26:39, 42.

[24] Mt 5:17-48; 7:12; 22:34-40.

[25] Mt 5:3-12, 17-20, 27-30; 6:1-18; 7:1-5, 13-14, 15-20, 21-23; 13:24-30, 36-43, 47-50; 18:5-6, 7-9.

[26] Mt 9:32-34; 12:22-24, 25-37, 38-45.

[27] Mt 5:20; 6:1-18.

disciples that the Pharisees are blind guides not to be followed
(15:12–14). And when he has answered the Pharisees' demand for a sign,
he tells his disciples to beware of their teaching (16:5–12). Such warnings
are addressed to Matthew's community, teaching them what attitude to
have toward Jamnia.

Matthew's anti-Pharisaism reaches its climax when Jesus teaches his
disciples and the crowds how their behavior should differ from that of the
scribes and Pharisees, then denounces his enemies as hypocrites and
blind guides, and finally laments over Jerusalem (23:1–39). The issues
named in the warnings are clear: "they preach, but do not practice. They
bind heavy burdens, hard to bear, and lay them on men's shoulders; but
they themselves will not move them with their finger. They do all their
deeds to be seen by men . . ." (23:3–5).[28] True followers of Jesus, however,
are not to be called rabbi, nor call any man their father, nor be called master. Rather they are to humble themselves and take on the role of a servant
(23:8–12). Such a stark contrast would enable the Matthean community
to understand how their behavior is to be patterned after that of Jesus
rather than that of the Jamnia scribes and Pharisees.

Matthean Community

The Gentile mission could never be successful if the Matthean
community did not learn to manage their internal confusion, tension,
conflict, and the divisive influence of false prophets. So the Matthean
Jesus invites his disciples, and at the same time the Evangelist invites
his community, to deepen their faith. Jesus calls them "men of little
faith" and attributes their inability to cure the possessed boy to their
lack of faith.[29] He also rebukes them for failing to understand his
warnings to and about the Pharisees.[30]

But the episodes in which the need for greater faith is most strikingly
taught are the calming of the storm at sea (8:18–27) and the walking on
the water (14:22–35). Prior to the first storm, the Matthean Jesus
commands the crowd around him to go over to the other side of the lake,
but only the disciples will follow him into the boat. Who are these
disciples, and how are they different from the rest of the crowd? Matthew

[28] Matthew does not totally discredit the scribes and Pharisees: "The scribes and
Pharisees sit on Moses' seat; so practice and observe whatever they tell you, but not what
they do" (Mt 23:2–3). This statement seems to contradict what Matthew has said about
Jesus as the authoritative teacher and interpreter of the Jewish law. I have no answer to this
contradiction, but only the suggestion that Matthew himself may not have arrived at a
consistent, well-thought-out understanding of how Jewish Christians were to relate to
Jamnia Pharisaism. Davies has commented: "Matthew reveals not a single, clearly defined
attitude towards Judaism but one that is highly complex and varied" (op. cit., p. 286).
[29] Mt 6:30; 8:26; 14:31; 16:8; 17:20.
[30] Mt 15:16–17; 16:8–11.

identifies them as those who are ready to share all that is implied in the fact that their master has no place to lay his head, and to put familial piety in second place when it conflicts with their commitment to follow Jesus (8:18–22). With the meaning of their action understood, the disciples follow Jesus into the boat. A storm rises, but Jesus is asleep. The disciples awaken him with an appeal for help: "Save, Lord; we are perishing." And Jesus responds with the question "Why are you afraid, O men of little faith?" (8:25–26). The disciples' inadequate faith refers to their lack of confidence in Jesus' power over the storm. But Matthew's readers, swamped by waves of opposition and conflict and with some beginning to lose heart, would easily identify with the disciples. Matthew calls for a deeper faith in Jesus' power over the evil symbolized by the storm at sea.[31]

Similarly, when Jesus walks through the storm to the disciples in the boat, he invites Peter to come to him on the water. Peter gets out of the boat, begins to walk toward Jesus, but then becomes afraid of the wind and begins to sink. Jesus catches him with the words "O man of little faith, why did you doubt?" (14:31). Once they are safe in the boat and the storm has ceased, the disciples worship Jesus with the profession "Truly you are the Son of God" (14:33). Once again Matthew intends his community to see their situation mirrored in the storm at sea, and their fears and doubts expressed in Peter's hesitation. He invites them to join the disciples in their renewed faith in Jesus as the Son of God.

Also through Jesus' instructions to his disciples Matthew addressed the confusion and conflict that was dividing his community. The Sermon on the Mount (5:1—7:28) and the so-called communitarian discourse (17:22—18:35) are the clearest examples. In the Sermon the disciples and the crowd are called "blessed" when they experience persecution and all kinds of evil (5:11–12). In the first antithesis they are warned against divisive anger and urged to reconciliation (5:21–26). In the fifth they are taught not to resist an evildoer (5:38–42). In the final antithesis Jesus instructs them to love even their enemies (5:43–48). The need for mutual forgiveness is expressed as a petition in the Our Father (6:12) and elaborated at the end of the prayer (6:14–15). Finally, in the epilogue Jesus warns against false prophets (7:15–20) and against those who would claim a place in the kingdom of heaven on the basis of mighty works in his name (7:21–23). Matthew's community could easily apply these instructions to their own confusion and conflicts and to the divisive influence of false prophets in their midst.[32]

---

[31] For further discussion see W. G. Thompson, "Reflections on the Composition of Mt 8:1—9:34," *Catholic Biblical Quarterly* 33 (1971) 371–74.

[32] For recent discussion of the problems confronting Matthew's community, see Harrington, "Matthean Studies since Joachim Rohde," pp. 379–80.

In the communitarian discourse in chapter 18, Matthew addresses the same issues, but against the background of Jesus' prediction of his own passion, death, and resurrection (17:22–23). His instructions concern attitudes and behavior among the disciples. If they would enter and achieve greatness in the future kingdom of heaven, they must now humble themselves like the child in their midst (18:1–4). Under no circumstances are they to weaken the faith of a fellow disciple through scandalous behavior (18:5–9). Instead, they should care for the one going astray and do everything possible to reconcile a brother who has wandered into sin (18:10–20). Finally, they are to forgive personal offenses without limit (18:21–35). Once again through these instructions Matthew teaches his community how to cope with their internal situation.[33]

Final Judgment

As a motivation for the Gentile mission, Matthew assured his readers that when the Son of Man comes, he will judge not only themselves but also the Gentiles to whom they are sent. In his perspective history will end with that final judgment. The righteous will enter the kingdom of heaven, and the unrighteous will be punished. It is not surprising, then, that in the final sections of Matthew's eschatological discourse Jesus describes the judgment of the disciples and the Gentiles.[34]

The Matthean Jesus exhorts his disciples to vigilance (24:36—25:30). He stresses the fact that, as the Son of Man, he will certainly come (24:37, 39, 43, 46; 25:6–7, 19), but also that his coming will be delayed (24:48; 25:5; also 25:19). Since the exact day and hour cannot be known, the disciples should watch and remain alert, like the faithful servant in his master's household or the virgins waiting for the bridegroom (24:36, 42, 44, 50; 25:13). When the Son of Man comes, however, the disciples will be divided one from another, like the men in the field or the women at the mill, like the faithful from the wicked servants, like the wise from the foolish virgins, or like the servants to whom the talents had been entrusted (24:40–41, 45–49; 25:2–4, 16–18). The reward will be great. The faithful servant will be set over all his master's possessions (24:47), the wise virgins enter the marriage feast (25:10), and the good and faithful servants enter into the joy of their master (25:20–23). But the punishment will be severe. The wicked servant will weep and gnash his teeth (24:51), the foolish virgins be excluded from the feast (25:11–12), and the slothful servant be cast into outer darkness (25:24–30). Finally, the criterion for judging the servants will be how faithful they were in carrying out their responsibilities (24:46–49). For the maidens it will be whether they are ready and watching at the bridegroom's coming (25:10, 13), and for servants entrusted with the talents it will be how well they made use of those talents (25:21, 23, 27).

Matthew addressed Jesus' words to his community in the aftermath of the Jewish war to correct the false impression that the end had already arrived and to call them to constant vigilance and readiness. He also wanted to motivate them to carry out the mission to all Gentiles. Merely belonging to the community would not guarantee entrance into the kingdom of heaven; for they will be judged on how well they used their different talents in the common task of "making disciples of all the Gentiles" (28:18) and in living with each other according to the law of love (22:34–40).

In the final scene, the judgment of the Gentiles (25:31–46), the Son of Man comes in his glory, the Gentiles are divided into the sheep and the goats, the sheep are rewarded and the goats are punished, and a clear criterion is expressed. Matthean scholars are more and more convinced that the Gentiles are being judged and that "the least of these my brethren" refers to the disciples sent to preach the gospel of the kingdom. The Gentiles will be judged by how well they treated the disciples. If they gave them food or drink, welcomed them or clothed them, or visited them in sickness or in prison, they will inherit the kingdom of heaven. But if they have turned their back on a disciple in need, they will be cast into eternal fire. For whether they know it or not, they were treating well or ill not only the disciples but also Jesus himself, who is one with his own.[35]

With this scene Matthew has assured his readers that when Jesus comes as the Son of Man, he will judge not only themselves but also the Gentiles to whom they are sent to preach the gospel of the kingdom. In this way he will be revealed as the universal and triumphant Lord over the entire world and all its inhabitants.

We have been describing how Matthew answered the question "Why the Church?" in his own language and in his own historical context, that is, in dialogue with both Jamnia Pharisaism and the needs of his community. He understood the nature and mission of the Church in

[35] Matthean scholars agree that this is the way Matthew understood the final-judgment scene (25:31–46), even though in the Christian tradition it has been read and interpreted to mean that all men, Christian and non-Christian alike, will be judged by their concern for the poor and underprivileged with whom Jesus is identified. See, e.g., Davies, *op. cit.*, pp. 97–98; L. Cope, "Matthew XXV:31–46—'The Sheep and the Goats' Reinterpreted," *Novum Testamentum* 11 (1969) 32–44; Lambrecht, "The Parousia Discourse," pp. 329–40; Thompson, "An Historical Perspective in the Gospel of Matthew," pp. 256–59.

terms of the mission of Jesus. During Jesus' earthly life that mission was limited to Israel. But in his death and resurrection Jesus gained universal authority over the entire world. Since he could no longer exercise that authority on earth, his mission to the Gentiles could be carried out only through his disciples. Hence the role of the Church, as Matthew saw it, was to preach the gospel of the kingdom to the Gentile world. It is the mission of the risen Jesus and the earthly Church in preparation for his second coming. Without the Church, then, the life, death, and resurrection of Jesus would have been without fulfilment in the world. This also meant that Jesus would be present to the Gentiles in his disciples and that he would judge the Gentiles by how they had treated his disciples.[36]

To support the Gentile mission, the Matthean community is to understand itself as a Christian movement no longer dependent upon Judaism but still rooted in Jesus Christ, the promised Jewish Messiah and the one authoritative teacher of the Jewish law. Internally, they are to deal decisively with the forces that divided them from one another by deepening their faith in Jesus and doing whatever is possible to avoid sin and introduce reconciliation and forgiveness. Finally, they are to look forward to Jesus' second coming, when, as the glorious and triumphant Son of Man, he will judge both themselves and all the Gentiles. With Matthew's understanding of the Church in mind, we now turn our attention to the Lukan writings to see how Luke responds to the same question about the Church.[37]

LUKE–ACTS

In several respects the situation addressed by the author of Luke–Acts is quite similar to that confronted by Matthew. First, the time of writing is roughly the same, namely, the mid-eighties of the first century. Secondly, the general region for the work's origin may well have been Syria. Thirdly, the church which he represented confronted a set of conditions calling for a new formulation of Christian identity. The

[36] The difference between this understanding of salvation for the Gentiles and recent theories about "anonymous Christianity" lies in the fact that the Gentiles must have contact with the disciples to be saved, whereas the anonymous Christian is saved without such contact.

[37] It is well to note connections between Matthew and the other articles in this issue. Matthew clearly connects the mission of Jesus and the mission of the Church. Within that spectrum Matthew would most probably agree with the first position presented by Schineller, namely, that Jesus Christ is the exclusive revealer and mediator of salvation, and the Church is the only way to salvation. Matthew does, however, place primary importance on the Gentile mission: see Haight's article on mission. Finally, Matthew sees the turning point of history as the death and resurrection of Jesus: see Sears's article on Trinitarian love as ground of the Church.

differences between the Matthean and Lukan social contexts, however, appear more fundamental than their similarities. First, Luke wrote for Christians who were predominantly of Gentile origin. Secondly, although the region of Antioch may have provided a basic stimulus, the author appears to have had in view many communities rather than one single community. Thirdly, the new situation which gave rise to his literary effort was not so clearly defined as in the case of Matthew. Whereas the latter faced an identity crisis precipitated by the Jewish reform of Jamnia, Luke confronted the historical distance between the Gentile churches of the eighties and their early Jewish origins. Awareness of temporal separation and *de facto* removal from socioreligious roots in Judaism, coupled with a need to confront ongoing history and assume a place in the Greco-Roman world, called for a clarification and a new affirmation of historical continuity.

As in the case of Matthew, these general statements must be substantiated by data from the Gospel itself. The task is facilitated by the nature of Luke's work, which is at once theological and historical, and by the author's two-volume arrangement. Unlike the other Evangelists, Luke materially distinguished the story of Jesus from that of the post-Easter communities and developed the story of the Church as the historical and temporal continuation of his earlier account (cf. Acts 1:1-2, 15). Consequently, it is far easier for us to discern his view of the Church's *raison d'être* as well as the Church's relationship to the life of Jesus. As we might expect of a well-integrated two-volume work, his account of Jesus' historical life presupposes and anticipates that of the Church, just as Acts reflects the concerns of the Gospel.

The dating of Luke–Acts in the mid-eighties is extremely helpful in clarifying the nature of the Lukan enterprise.[38] Unlike Matthew, however, where a similar dating enables the scholar to see the relation between the Gospel and a specific historical event, namely, the work at

---

[38] The approximate dating of Luke–Acts in the eighties is founded on a number of observations. First, the work's use of Mark's Gospel presupposes the existence of that Gospel, as well as a post-Markan course of events of sufficient duration to seriously date this earlier work and to require a new synthesis of the Christian reality (Lk 1:1-4). Further, Luke's separation of the destruction of Jerusalem and the dispersal of the Jews (Lk 21:5-24) from his account of the end of the world (Lk 17:22-37; 21:25-28) presupposes that a number of years have passed since the Jewish war and that this event is no longer viewed apocalyptically (cf. Lk 17:20-21). On the other hand, the picture of Christian diffusion presented in Acts, while positing the existence of many communities, does not presuppose strong bonds between the churches. Indeed, the term *ekklēsia* refers to individual congregations and not to a universal Church. Only in Acts 9:31 does it have a somewhat broader extension when it refers to the church in Judea, Galilee, and Samaria. These considerations, when buttressed by other indications to be given below, appear sufficient to situate Luke–Acts some time in the eighties.

Jamnia, it is the temporal distance between the time of writing and the origins of the Gospel in the life of Jesus which is here significant. In part, the problem to which Luke intended to respond had been created by the very passage of time.

A geographical locus for Luke–Acts which is at least roughly related to that of Matthew may be argued from their common use of Mark and Q as sources, from the fact that both provided their Gospels with infancy narratives, appearance stories, Jesus' genealogy, and closely-related developments of the temptations of Jesus. However differently each Evangelist may have approached and developed these materials, the very fact of their incorporation in both Gospels presupposes a set of common concerns and related approaches to Christian realities. Since neither appears to have influenced the other literarily, the relationship is best accounted for in terms of a related geographical and historical *Sitz im Leben*. Luke's concern with the role and place of Antioch in early Christian history points us strongly in the direction of that city, as does his use of a liturgical tradition related to that cited by Paul in 1 Cor 11:23–25.[39]

Luke's concern with the predominantly Gentile churches can be seen from his outline of Christianity's movement out of its Judean cradle into the greater Gentile world. The progress was indicated by the scattering of Hellenistic Jewish Christians from Jerusalem (Acts 8:1; 11:19–20) and their gradual expulsion from the synagogues of the Diaspora. Although Peter himself was credited with a primordial role in opening the Christian message to the Gentiles (Acts 10:1—11:18; 15:7), Paul was the apostle to the Gentiles par excellence (Acts 9:15; 15:3, 12; 22:21), a fact indicated literarily by the author's manner of referring to Saul Paul. Whereas in the early chapters of Acts he consistently referred to him as Saul, beginning with 13:9 he uses the Gentile designation Paul. These observations are supported by data from the Gospel such as the genealogy of Jesus, which unlike that of Matthew does not begin with Abraham (Mt 1:1–2) but reaches back to Adam (Lk 3:38) and by Simeon's prophetic word to Jesus' parents (Lk 2:32).

The concern of Acts with the sweep of Christianity through Phoenicia, Cyprus, Syria, Asia Minor, and the Aegean basin all the way to the Roman capital indicates the breadth of the author's concerns. Although

---

[39] In 1 Cor 11:23 Paul indicates that what he handed on to the Christians of Corinth, i.e., circa 52 A.D., he had previously received. The statement thus refers us back in time to Paul's stay at Antioch, which was the mother community of Pauline missions. Several of the differences between the Lukan and the Pauline Eucharistic text may be accounted for in terms of development in liturgical forms employed at Antioch. The two would thus have quoted from the Antiochene tradition at different moments in the latter's development. This is not to deny additional Markan influences on the Lukan text.

Antioch looms large in the background, it would be wrong to present Luke as addressing himself primarily to the Gentile-Christian community of that city. Rather should we speak of him as a man of the Hellenistic Christian mission.[40] This fact differentiates him from Matthew, who spoke out of and addressed a particular community which we label Matthean. The difference may be accounted for in terms of the very nature of Gentile-Christian communities, which did not emerge out of prior well-defined communities as in the case of a Jewish-Christian community. A Gentile Church could only reflect the Gentile world, where a measure of local civic cohesion may be evidenced, but whose members related far more readily to the broad sociopolitical realities of the Roman world. In other words, the more universalist *Sitz im Leben* of Luke-Acts was but a reflection of the Gentile world from which its addressees were largely derived. In Luke, the universal mission was thus not a program to be undertaken by a particular community but a datum of early Christian history to be assimilated and ordered.

As in the case of Matthew, the very existence of Luke's Gospel indicates awareness of a need to address the Christian community with a new synthesis of the gospel. The preface to Luke–Acts (Lk 1:1–4) attests to Luke's conscious intention in this regard. The Lukan context which we have outlined to this point, however, shows that Luke's situation was vastly different from that of Matthew. For one, while both Matthew and Luke needed to establish the Church's relationship to Judaism, the former spoke from a community which continued to define itself in relation to and even as quasi-parallel to the greater Jewish community of which it could no longer form a part. The Lukan situation, on the other hand, shows greater distance from Judaism, which no longer acted as a contemporary threat or even as a point of reference. The Judaism to which Lukan churches had to relate was a phenomenon which reflected the historical origins of these churches and not a Judaism which they now needed to encounter. This situation merely provided a different kind of identity problem, one stemming from the communities' felt distance from their historical origins. The clearest and most general evidence for this problem lies in the very nature of Luke's work as historical. In this respect, the following pages will develop the Lukan problematique as one of demonstrating Hellenistic Christianity's continuity with its origins.

Luke's historical perspective was also influenced by the context of the Gentile Church, in which Christians did not see the Roman world as a threat. Consequently, the urgent expectation of an imminent Parousia,

[40] The Hellenistic Christian mission was the product of Jewish Christians whose origins lay in the Hellenistic Diaspora. In Luke's time, at least in the Lukan communities, it had become the missionary effort of Gentile Christians to the Hellenistic world.

which had been characteristic of Mark's Gospel and of traditions held in common by Matthew and Luke, was tempered with terms such as "daily," thereby indicating the author's commitment to ongoing history.[41] Since such history could hardly be divorced from the Greco-Roman world, we are not surprised to find that Romans are accorded a singularly sympathetic treatment throughout Luke–Acts. The Lukan context thus reveals a Christianity which must identify itself not only in terms of its Jewish origins but also in relation to its position in the Roman world. Luke's view of the Church within his response to this complex need constitutes the object of the following inquiry.

Our study treats first of Luke's understanding of the Church in relation to the continuum of history. In this first section, historico-temporal considerations appear primary, and our analysis focuses on the life of the Church as a moment in Luke's theology of history. We shall then analyze Luke's view of the Church's role within its historical period. In this second section, historico-social considerations become primary, and our analysis bears both on the internal life of the Church and on the Church's mission vis-à-vis the non-Christian world.

The Church in the Continuum of History

The fact that Luke presented the gospel in a history represents an extremely significant development in that it clearly witnesses to Christianity's need to take temporality seriously. In Luke–Acts, the Church and its gospel has a prehistory and a past as well as a future; its life unfolds in the present. Moreover, this Church exists in a historical period which it partially defines and which forms one segment of a much longer historical continuum. Although the author's primary concern is with the continuum of biblical history, he is also careful to situate John the Baptist and Jesus in the history of the Roman Empire.[42] One of the preconditions for such a historical presentation lies in the recognition that the Church has a future. Apart from an effort to formulate the Church's ongoing role in history, the subordinate effort to establish the Church's continuity with the past would be meaningless.

In order to circumscribe the Church's place in history, we must take careful note of Luke's division of history. Conzelmann, more than any other, has made the scholarly world aware of Luke's ordering of history: first, there was the time of John the Baptist, in whom the history of Israel found its culmination; second, there was the time of Jesus' ministry, which constitutes the center of salvation history; and third, there was the time of the Church, which followed upon Jesus' ascension and will

---

[41] Compare Lk 11:3 with Mt 6:11, and Lk 9:23 with Mk 8:34.
[42] Cf. E. A. LaVerdiere, "John the Prophet: Jesus' Forerunner in Luke's Theology of History," *The Bible Today*, March 1975, pp. 323–24, 328–29.

endure until the end of time.[43] Conzelmann's division, however, stands in need of further refinement, since both the time of Jesus and that of the Church are united by Luke in one era of the Spirit, which stands distinct from the era of Israel and John the Baptist. Accordingly, Luke saw history as divided into two major eras, the pre-Christian era of Israel and the Christian era. Further, the latter was subdivided into two periods, that of Jesus, which was inaugurated by the descent of the Spirit at his baptism and culminated in his resurrection-ascension, and that of the Church, which began with the Spirit's descent at Pentecost to endure until the *eschaton*. This division is required by the manifest parallelism between the two descents of the Spirit. In Jesus' case, the Spirit's descent serves to interpret his baptism (Lk 3:21–22); in the case of the Church, the descent of the Spirit is itself interpreted as a baptism (Acts 1:5). The time of Jesus and the time of the Church are thus extremely closely related.

While affirming the generic unity of these two times, however, we must not minimize their distinction, which is so clearly indicated by the two ascension narratives (Lk 24:50–53; Acts 1:6–11) and even by Luke's attribution of a farewell discourse to Jesus (Lk 22:14–38). Literary data such as this points to the definitiveness of the end of Jesus' life or *exodos* (Lk 9:31) at Jerusalem and the new beginning which follows his ascension.

Both the distinction and the close relationship between the time of Jesus and the time of the Church are significant for Luke's ecclesiology, in that Jesus and the Church belong to one and the same era. The historical life of Jesus was not purely and simply relegated to the past. On the contrary, the retelling of his life and message has immediate bearing on that of the post-Easter Christians, a Lukan concern evidenced by the very existence of his first volume and his abundant use of discourses, which in the manner of Greek and Jewish Hellenistic historians enable the author to address Jesus' message to new historical situations.

For Luke, then, the Church lives in continuity with the life and work of Jesus. Literarily, this continuity is indicated by the parallelism between the Gospel's presentation of the life of Jesus from Galilee to Jerusalem and Acts' delineation of the development and spread of the Church from Jerusalem to Rome. Theologically, it is articulated by means of the principle of prophetic necessity, which is Luke's application of the early Christian method of reflecting on events according to the Scriptures. The same principle enables Luke to relate the Christian era to Israel and John the Baptist, whom Luke presents primarily as a prophet and only secondarily as a baptist.[44]

[43] Hans Conzelmann, *The Theology of St. Luke* (New York, 1960) pp. 12–15.
[44] LaVerdiere, *art. cit.*, pp. 323–30.

   Although it is the work of the Spirit that serves most strikingly to set
Luke and Acts in a parallel relationship, many other literary indications
could be adduced. Among these, perhaps the most significant is the
manner in which the latter part of both works is presented as a long
journey narrative. Each of these is marked by a very clear and deliberate
beginning. In Lk 9:51 we read that when the days drew near for Jesus to
be taken up, he set out for Jerusalem. This journey to Jerusalem ended
only with his ascension. It is thus a theological journey as well as a
geographical one, and Jerusalem is seen at once as a geographical
terminus as well as a symbol of Jesus' passage to God. In Acts 19:21 we
read that Paul resolved in the Spirit to go through Macedonia and Achaia
to Jerusalem, adding that afterwards he must also see Rome. From that
point on, the indicated journey provides a loose cadre for the remainder
of Acts, which ends with Paul at Rome. As with Jerusalem, Rome is at
once a geographical point and a symbol. In this case, however, the city is
symbolic not of an end but of the universal nature of the mission which
continues into Luke's own time (Acts 1:8) and will go on until Jesus'
return (Acts 1:11) at a humanly undetermined and undeterminable
moment (Acts 1:7).
   Luke's methodological use of a unifying theological principle to relate
the period of the Church to that of Jesus is best observed in Lk 24:7,
25–27, 44–47, where we find both the characteristic Lukan term *dei* and
explicit mention of the prophets and the Scriptures. In these three sets of
verses we note a definite progression towards a more ample and
comprehensive application of the principle.[45] As we might expect, Lk
24:44–47, which is situated in the Gospel's final pericope, presents Luke's
most highly developed expression of prophetic necessity. Both the events
of the end of Jesus' life, including his resurrection, and the mission of the
Church to all nations are said to be according to the Scriptures.
Moreover, Jesus himself had indicated the necessity of this biblical fulfilment. Luke thus situated Jesus in the realm of prophetic fulfilment
as well as in that of prophetic promise, the latter with regard to future
events in his own life and mission which would then be continued in that
of the Church. As fulfilment, the two periods of the Christian era of the
Spirit, which is that of the preaching of the good news of God's kingdom,
were also related to John the Baptist, who terminated the era of the law
and the prophets (cf. Lk 16:16a).
   On the basis of the above general outline of Luke's historical
perspective, it is now possible to situate the Church with greater
historico-temporal precision, first with regard to the past in Jesus'

---

[45] Cf. Paul Schubert, "The Structure and Significance of Luke 24," in *Neutestament-
liche Studien für Rudolf Bultmann* (Berlin, 1954) pp. 165–86.

mission and the Church's Jewish origins, and second in relation to the future. As we have already noted, Luke saw the work of Jesus and the Church as universal from the very start (Lk 2:32; 3:23-38). In the passage which announces the beginning of the Galilean ministry (Lk 4:16-30), a unit which not only refers to a single incident but is proleptic and programmatic with regard to the remainder of the work, the author presented Jesus' own intention as universal. Alluding to biblical precedent (1 K 17:9; 2 K 5:1-14), Jesus challenges the Nazareth synagogue with the Gentile mission (Lk 4:25-27). In the Gospel, however, save for incidental contacts with Gentiles, this intention remains unfulfilled. *De facto*, Jesus' historical mission was to Jews, and so Luke presented it. Universal in intent, his mission remained geographically, temporally, and ethnically limited and incomplete in execution. The Church's role would be to continue Jesus' mission by extending it beyond the historical limits of Jesus' career and by eventually bringing his intention to fulfilment. In this way the Church's mission (Lk 24:47) could actually be presented as the fulfilment of what had been written about Jesus himself (Lk 24:44).[46]

In its life and mission the Church is also dominated by Christ's future return. Jesus, who has ascended into heaven, will come again in the same way as the apostolic community has seen him go (Acts 1:11). The Church's mission does not represent an absolute reality completely understandable in itself, but one which is relative to the prior historical life of Jesus as well as to his future coming. Continuing Christ's work during his historical absence, it prepares mankind for his eventual return. Thus it is that, from the point of view of the Spirit, we must speak of continuity between the time of the Church and that of Jesus. In a Christological perspective, however, we find the Church living in a new period which is relative to that of Christ by reason of both its origins and its future consummation.

By situating the Church in a history of the work of the Spirit, as the expression of prophetic fulfilment and in the context of Jesus' intended universal mission, Luke has responded to the need of the Gentile Church of the eighties to clarify its relationship to its Jewish origins and to the historical life and work of Jesus. He has thus enabled the Church to integrate its self-understanding with regard to the years of post-Easter experience, which had led Hellenistic communities far from their Jewish origins. On this basis these communities could then address themselves to the long-term continuation of Christ's mission. Looking forward to Christ's return, they were nevertheless free of immediate apocalyptic pressure.

---

[46] So, too, our understanding of the Church's mission depends on our understanding of Christ's mission today; cf. Schneller's article in this issue.

The Church within Its Own Period of History

The notion of salvation history provided Luke with a broad temporal framework for the Church's *raison d'être*. Indeed, the acceptance of ongoing history as theologically meaningful is absolutely essential to Luke's view of the Church. Without such acceptance, salvation history would have ended with the death of Jesus, and the life of the Church would have unfolded purely as a period of waiting for Christ's return. His resurrection would have been significant for the life of Jesus himself and as a condition for his return. Apart from providing a sign of hope for Jesus' followers, however, it would not have been a factor in the life of the Church. Salvation history was consequently an element intrinsic to the very nature of the Church, and we may state that in the most general terms the Church's *raison d'être* was to be God's historical agent in the ongoing work of salvation.

Having examined the Church's generic temporal purpose, we now turn to Luke's presentation of the Church's specific function within its own historical period. In this respect the Church may be said to have a bipolar orientation. As a community of sharing, it is characterized by the strong personal bonds of its members. As a community of witness, it is actively engaged in a mission to those still outside the pale of the gospel.

The Church is a community of sharing, and as such its sociohistorical *raison d'être* revolves around its own internal existence and set of relationships. This is the picture of the Church which emerges from Acts, and in particular from the major Lukan summaries of life in the primitive Jerusalem community (2:42–47; 4:32–35). These summary statements, which are even more concisely summarized in Acts 2:42, are paradigmatic of the ideal life of the Church. Like the parent Christian community at Jerusalem, a Christian community can and should be identified as one which devotes itself to the teaching of the apostles, to koinonia, that is, fellowship, brotherhood, common life, and sensitivity, to sharing in the breaking of bread and to the prayers characteristic of the community.

The four descriptive elements included in Acts 2:42 incorporate various aspects of the Church's life as it is presented throughout Luke–Acts. First, Luke's synthesis and interpretation of the teaching of the apostles is repeatedly presented in the various apostolic discourses of Acts, and in a sense Luke–Acts as a whole may be assumed under this rubric, since it is given as an effort at deeper and authentic understanding of Christian life and tradition (Lk 1:1–4; Acts 1:1–5). It should be noted that apostolic teaching does not consist primarily in presenting the message of Jesus but the Resurrection event in which Jesus' life culminated. Second, Christian koinonia, which includes a measure of material sharing of goods, is developed in Acts 4:32–35 and in the two pericopes which follow. Barnabas' action is a positive example of the ideal (Acts 4:36–37); that of Ananias and Sapphira is a negative response or breach of brotherhood (Acts 5:1–11). This last indicates that koinonia had become problematic in the Christian communities addressed by Luke and points to the idealizing nature of Luke's picture of the earliest community. The theme is also reflected in the strong sense of hospitality which pervades relationships between Jesus and his fellow men. Third, the breaking of bread and the spirit of early Eucharistic meals is frequently presented in Luke–Acts. The account of Paul's departure from Troas serves as a good example (Acts 20:7–12). By focusing on Eutychus' near-fatal experience, the passage emphasizes the life-giving nature of the Christian assembly. Fourth, the importance of prayer is noted in Acts' first brief summary (Acts 1:14) as the characteristic attitude of the apostolic community even as it sought to establish itself after the events of the Passion and as it awaited the gift of the Spirit. Indeed, the role of prayer in the life of Jesus and his followers is one of the more general themes of Luke–Acts. The prayer of Jesus at the Mount of Olives is actually given as a short catechesis on Christian prayer (Lk 22:39–46), as is Lk 11:1–13, which includes the Lukan tradition of the Lord's Prayer (vv. 2–4).

The Church's internal existence is inseparable from Christ's presence to its members. In Lk 24:13–35 we read the story of two disciples who come to recognize the risen Lord in the breaking of bread. This paradigmatic narrative develops the relationship between the disciples' experience of the unrecognized Lord in a discussion on the way to Emmaus and their recognition of him in a meal at Emmaus (Lk 24:32). The passage from nonrecognition to recognition is mediated by their invitation that Jesus remain with them (Lk 24:29). The Emmaus narrative's main intention is to present the locus and conditions for the recognition of the risen Lord.[47] This locus is specified as the Christian fellowship meal or breaking of bread. The main conditions are twofold. On the one hand, there is the initiative of Jesus himself; on the other, the disciples' response in their invitation that Jesus remain with them. We may safely assume that the story was told in response to Jesus' continuing historical absence and its perception as a loss to Jesus' followers. The significance of the Emmaus unit is thus inseparable from Luke's theology of the Ascension. Since Jesus can be experienced and recognized in an entirely new manner, which later generations would term sacramental, the absence of the historical Jesus (Lk 24:31b, 50–53) does not leave the Christians in dis-

---

[47] The intention of the narrative is most easily seen from the author's use of a literary inclusion in vv. 16 and 31 and from the concluding summary statement in v. 35.

tressful sadness (Lk 24:18). On the contrary, they are filled with a joy
which must be shared (24:32–35) and which expresses itself in divine
praise (24:52–53).

Luke's understanding of the Church's internal social life is thus clearly
related to the presence of Christ. Nearly all the elements included in the
summary statement of Acts 2:42–47 have been assumed in the narrative
statement of Lk 24:13–35. In terms of Luke's theology, we may consequently assert that the Church is a community whose life and existence is
justified, at least in part, by the fact that knowing and experiencing
Christ's presence has value.[48] Hence, the question "Why the Church?" is
inseparable from the prior question "Why Jesus Christ?" Although the
former question arises from the account of Acts and the Easter narrative
of Lk 24, it can only be answered in reference to Luke's narrative of Jesus'
historical life as presented in Lk 1–23. Luke's own manner of presenting
Jesus in light of the Church's future life attests to the methodological
soundness of such an inquiry.

At several points in the Gospel the significance of Christ's presence to
men is presented in terms of salvation. Such is the case, for example, in
the story of Zacchaeus (Lk 19:1–10), which like the Emmaus account is
structurally articulated by means of a literary inclusion. After a
narrative introduction, we read in 19:5 that today Jesus will stay at
Zacchaeus' house. In 19:9 the account climaxes with the statement that
today salvation has come to his house. The author has thus identified
the presence of Jesus with the presence of salvation. Correlatively, the
hosting of Jesus is equivalent to the hosting of salvation. The theme's
importance may be seen from its earlier prominence in the Lukan
prologue's birth narrative (cf. 2:11, 30). Concretely, Jesus' salvific presence is expressed in his attitude of service, which in its contrast with the
great of this world provides an example for Jesus' disciples (Lk 22:24–30).

The Church's internal set of Christian relationships can be seen as the
community's *manière d'être* rather than its *raison d'être*. In actual fact,
the two are intimately related. Luke does not present the Church's
mission as directed exclusively to non-Christians, but also as addressed
to its own members, who remain in continuous need of Christ's salvific
presence (cf. Lk 22:31–34).[49] The purpose of the Church is thus to provide
a living and active locus of Christ's presence to followers of Jesus, who are
ever on the way. Concretely, this function is epitomized in the breaking
of bread, which in Acts 27:21–26, 33–38 is presented precisely in its
relationship to salvation. As with the historical Jesus, the attitude of
Christians and in particular of Church leaders must be one of service.

In terms of its mission to the world, the Church may be described as a

---

[48] Cf. Sears's article in this issue.   [49] Cf. *ibid.*

community of witness.[50] Such is the most obvious function of the Church as it is presented throughout the course of Acts in both narrative and discourse. Christians witness to others concerning Christ's work, but especially concerning what God has done in Jesus' behalf and through him on behalf of others.

This second aspect of the Church's *raison d'être* is intimately related to the first, which presented the Church in relation to its own internal life. Nowhere is this point more clearly asserted than in Acts 10:40–43, where the witnesses are said to be precisely those Christians who ate and drank with Jesus after he rose from the dead. This reference to Christian meals with the risen Lord must be related to the account of Emmaus, whose significance we have already indicated, and to other meal contexts in Luke–Acts.

As with regard to the Church's own experience of the risen Lord, the value of the Church's witness to Christ stands justified by the fact that Christ's work and message had value. Consequently, the question "Why the Church?" is once again inseparable from the prior question "Why the mission of Jesus?" In answer to the latter question, we once again turn to Lk 4:14–30, which is Luke's introductory statement concerning the mission of Christ, and in which Christ's work is presented as the proclamation of the good news through word and action, initially to Jews but ultimately to Gentiles. The content and nature of the mission is summarized in the text of Is 61:1 f., which is applicable to both Christ and the Church. Following the rejection of Christ's message by the Jews, Luke has the historical Jesus announce the mission to the Gentiles. Acts presents the Church as commissioned to carry out this mission, which remained unfulfilled at the time of Jesus' death. The story of Cornelius (Acts 10) is given as fundamental to the development of the Church's Gentile mission. As the turning point in the execution of the gospel mission, it also points to difficulties in the Church's assumption of a universal role. Indirectly, it thus attests to the redactional nature of the universal missionary program set out in Luke–Acts.

Thus has Luke confronted the Church's ongoing existence as well as its mission to the Gentiles. Following Jesus' death, the Christian communities continue to live in his presence. Filled with his Spirit, they carry out his mission to the ends of the earth.

CONCLUSION

With Matthew and Luke in hand, we can now offer some tentative suggestions as to what these writings might mean today and how they might function as normative for the Church today. That Church is

[50] Haight stresses this dimension of the Church.

experiencing a radical change, the type of change that leads to a new self-understanding and calls for new patterns of behavior toward the modern world. Matthew and Luke both wrote for Christian communities in transition. So we suggest that in spite of the temporal, geographical, and cultural gap between their situations and ours, we can affirm strong correlations in terms of the dynamics of change.

Those dynamics can be briefly described. First, events break in upon the community, causing its members to question their current behavior (Are we doing the right thing?) and even their own identity (Who are we?). Such questions trigger a sense of disorientation, confusion, tension, and often lead to conflict, as different people respond very differently to the changing situation. Some want to hang on to the past, cut out what no longer fits, and put new life in traditional patterns of behavior. Others want to accommodate the past, adjust to the new situation, facilitate growth and development, but always in harmony with the past. Still others want to break cleanly with the past, create unique solutions, and introduce a total transformation or revolution.[51] Such pluralism and confusion drive the community back to its roots, to the persons and experiences from which it came to birth, so that they can rediscover and reclaim those persons and events. Then and only then can they meet the present and creatively address its challenges. Exploring their past enables them to formulate a more appropriate self-understanding, to create new perspectives from which to view their changed situations, and finally to choose more effective patterns of behavior and strategies for action.

Change was introduced to Matthew and his largely Jewish-Christian community by the events of the Jewish war, principally the destruction of Jerusalem and the Temple, and by the emergence of Jamnia Pharisaism. These events made them wonder how they should behave toward their fellow Jews and how they should understand themselves in relation to Judaism and to the non-Jewish world. Such questions caused confusion, tension, and conflict in the Matthean community, a situation that was intensified by the activity of false prophets. So Matthew's task was to reaffirm their roots in Jesus Christ and through him in their Jewish heritage, and at the same time to teach them how to respond to their present situation. He accomplished this task by retelling the life of Jesus. In his earthly ministry the Matthean Jesus revealed himself to be the Jewish Messiah and the sole authoritative teacher of the Jewish law. His mission was limited to Israel. But after his death and resurrection the same Jesus, now endowed with universal authority, sends his disciples

    [51] John W. O'Malley, "Reform, Historical Consciousness, and Vatican II's Aggiornamento," THEOLOGICAL STUDIES 32 (1971) 573–601, esp. pp. 594–95.

to the Gentile world with the assurance that he will be with them to the end. Matthew thus taught his community that they must continue to exist, that they must understand themselves as separate and distinct from Jamnia Judaism, and that they must focus their attention on the Gentile mission. They must, in a word, choose to become universalist rather than remain sectarian, since only in so doing would they become in fact the true Israel, by carrying out the mission of their risen Lord. To accept this new self-understanding and fulfil their mission, they must deepen their faith in Jesus Christ and work toward reconciliation and forgiveness within the community.

Change had a very different meaning for Luke and the predominantly Gentile-Christian communities for whom he wrote. The widespread success of the universal Gentile-Christian mission was a matter of history, and the Lukan communities reflected the broad sociopolitical realities of the Greco-Roman world. Judaism was not part of their contemporary culture, but it was at the roots of the Christianity to which the Gentiles had been converted. So the Gentile converts had many questions about how they should behave and understand themselves as Christians. Luke's task, consequently, was to demonstrate how Hellenistic Christianity was to see itself in relation to Jesus of Nazareth, in relation to the Jewish-Christian communities from which it came, and also in relation to its present position in the Greco-Roman world. He accomplished it in a two-volume work in which the life of Jesus and the story of the early Church were united in one era of the Spirit and presented as two phases of the one period of biblical history. For Luke, the Hellenistic-Christian communities live in continuity with the life and work of Jesus, a continuity delineated by the geographical movement of the narrative and explained theologically as according to God's necessary plan for the world. Unlike Matthew, Luke saw the work of Jesus and the Church as universal from the outset. Jesus' mission was universal in intent but incomplete in execution. It belonged to the Church to continue that mission, bringing his intention to fulfilment in preparation for his eventual return. Within its own historical period, then, the Church had been and was to continue to be a community of sharing characterized by strong personal bonds among its members, and a community of witness actively engaged in the universal mission begun by Jesus during his earthly life. The Hellenistic-Christian converts addressed by Luke could easily come to see themselves as full-fledged members of such a community.

Change in the Church today means confronting the modern world and the events that shape our understanding of the world.[52] The result is an

---

[52] For a description of this problem, see Haight's article in this issue.

almost despairing confusion. Within Roman Catholicism, for example, we have become increasingly aware, in the words of John O'Malley, that Vatican II "is an inadequate expression of what is required today and, indeed, of what is actually happening today. We are not experiencing a 'reform' as that term is traditionally understood as a correction, or revival, or development, or even updating. We are experiencing a transformation, even a revolution."[53]

Can the writings of Matthew and Luke inform and influence the Church as we address this common task? How can they function as normative for the Church in this time of change? We must affirm once again the enormous distance that separates their situation from our own.[54] But within those differences we suggest three normative correlations. First, in a time of change a new understanding of the Church and its mission must be developed out of a new understanding of Jesus Christ and his mission; for both Matthew and Luke see the Church as the necessary extension and continuation of the work of Jesus.[55] Second, an adequate understanding of the Church must focus on its universal mission. Matthew's community had to face the decision not to remain sectarian but to become universal, because otherwise the universal mission of their risen Lord would not become a reality on earth. Luke's communities understood that Jesus' mission was universal from the outset, but that they were charged with the task of bringing it to fulfilment. Both affirm universalism, thereby suggesting that in any time of change the Church must come to understand itself in the terms of its broad, universal mission to the non-Christian world.[56] Finally, concern must also be shown for the inner life of the Church. Matthew was concerned that the tension, conflict, and confusion dividing his community be healed, but clearly in function of the Gentile mission. Luke seems to have made concern for the community's inner life more central. But both see it connected to the mission to the world.[57] So we suggest that this concern is normative for the changing Church today.

As a final word, we would like to suggest that the theologians' task today is not unlike that of the Evangelists. They must listen to the past and speak to the present and the future. For the Evangelists, the past was the life of Jesus and the early Church and the more remote history of Israel, and they spoke to the present in stories about Jesus and the Church. Theologians today have a far more difficult task. The past is far

[53] *Art. cit.*, p. 601.

[54] Recall pp. 24-25 above.

[55] This conclusion supports the approach to the Church taken in this series of articles; see Schineller.

[56] Haight stresses this role of the Church.

[57] Sears agrees more with the Lukan perspective.

more diversified, and the present far more complex.[58] Today we speak several languages at once: the descriptive language of the Bible, the technical language of creed and doctrinal statement, and the more precise language of contemporary science. Nevertheless, the process of listening and speaking remains the same. It is our hope that by describing and interpreting the data from Matthew and Luke, and by offering some suggestions as to its normative contribution to the Church today, we have assisted Christian theologians as they face the question "Why the Church?"

[58] The patristic article by Burns illustrates how diverse that past has been. For a discussion of our present situation, see David Tracy, *Blessed Rage for Order* (New York, 1975) pp. 3–21.

III

THE ECONOMY OF SALVATION: TWO PATRISTIC TRADITIONS

J. PATOUT BURNS, S.J.

Jesuit School of Theology in Chicago

IN THE ANALYSIS of the New Testament materials advanced by William Thompson and Eugene LaVerdiere, the authors of the Matthean and Lukan writings are understood as theologians who interpreted the life of Christ and the beginnings of the Church in a way which met the questions and problems of their own day.[1] This process of interpretation continued in other forms and is recorded in the writings of the Fathers. As the Christian community entered into conversation with and gradually dominated Mediterranean civilization, these men attempted to explain the message and significance of Christ in the language of the new culture, submitting to its demands for cosmological rather than historical explanations and drawing heavily on its philosophy, especially its anthropology. The Fathers regarded Scripture as the norm of their theology, but gradually realized that they could not be limited by the vocabulary or the explanatory categories of the Scriptures.[2]

The carefully constructed definitions and creeds of the ecumenical councils rather than the theological explanations of the Fathers are the normative documents from this age. Still, the writings of the Fathers attained an authority which made them resources for scholastic syntheses and Reformation debate, as well as the contemporary renewal of theology.[3] The Fathers legitimated the theological process, established faith's right to seek understanding, for Christians who considered the normative Scriptures historical reports and revelations whose very language was part of their content. By attempting to transpose the gospel into explanatory language, the Fathers also established paradigms for subsequent thought. They explored the various ways of thinking about creation and fall, redemption and salvation, and indicated the implications for Christian life of one or another understanding.

My purpose in this study is neither to judge contemporary theologies by patristic standards nor to indicate the patristic anticipation of contemporary questions. I intend, rather, to extract from the patristic materials certain schemas in which they attempted to understand the Christian economy of salvation. By examining the work of representative

---

[1] "New Testament Communities in Transition" above.

[2] One finds a justification of this breaking out of scriptural categories in Athanasius' defense of the use of the term *Homoousios*.

[3] One recalls not only the *Glossa ordinaria* and the *Libri sententiarum* of Lombard, but the *Catalogus testium veritatis* of Flacius, the *De theologicis dogmatibus* of Petavius, and "La nouvelle théologie" of this century.

Fathers, we can uncover the foundations, the internal logic, and the implications of certain ways of thinking about the process of salvation. Thus we may clarify the resources and limitations of each paradigm of the economy of salvation.

First I shall explain the tendencies of the Latin and Greek traditions and the categories in which I propose to analyze them. Then I shall describe the economy of salvation as it is explained by Gregory of Nyssa and Augustine. Finally I shall generalize and define two different schemas and reflect upon their value for contemporary theology.

TWO ECONOMIES OF SALVATION

In the ancient Church we find two significantly different explanations of the economy of creation and salvation. A tradition of Greek thought which began in Justin Martyr, developed in Origen, and achieved orthodox expression in Gregory of Nyssa stressed the general availability of the means of terrestrial and heavenly salvation and a developmental continuity from birth to beatitude. These theologians recognized a universal operation of Christ and found in the Church the fulness of his effective presence.[4] Moreover, both Origen and Gregory asserted that all whom God had created would finally be saved in Christ.

The orientation of Latin theology contradicts this Greek universalism. Tertullian, Cyprian, and their Roman counterparts appear to have assumed that the salvation accomplished in Jesus Christ could be attained only through his Church. A person passes from sin to salvation by fulfilling the conditions which God imposes for participation in Christ's redemption rather than by developing the potentialities with which every one was gifted in creation. Thus one must believe the teaching of Christ, receive baptism, and belong to the communion of the proper Church in order to be freed from sin and raised to the glory of Christ.[5] This theological tradition finds its fullest elaboration in Augustine, who carefully specified the conditions which God has set down and the reasons for their necessity.

The Greek and Latin traditions differ in their paradigms of the passage to beatitude. Origen and Gregory concentrate on the gradual development of the human soul, which is freed from bondage to earthly delights and rises to union with God.[6] The ascetic life provides the primary analogate of the way of salvation, and Antony of Egypt's vision of

[4] Justin, e.g., speaks of the Word as the universal source of moral reason, of Christ's teaching as the fullest expression of this reasonableness, and of Christians as the most reasonable and wisdom-loving of humans. See 1 Apology 46, 63; 2 Apology 8, 10, 13.

[5] Tertullian's insistence on Montanist asceticism in obedience to the Paraclete and Cyprian's defense of rebaptism are indications of this attitude. See Cyprian, Epp. 69–75.

[6] Even in the Exhortation to Martyrdom Origen stresses the liberation of the human spirit and the degrees of glory which correspond to the intensity of suffering and love. See chaps. 15, 42, 47.

purified souls evading the snares of Satan in their ascent to heaven symbolizes the aspirations of this culture and its theology.[7] Both Origen and Gregory offer allegorical commentaries on the Canticle of Canticles in which they describe the soul's mystical union with God. In contrast, the Latins emphasize the definitive divine intervention which raises the faithful Christian from death and translates him to glory. The martyr who struggles in the arena to persevere in confessing Christ looks to an immediate deliverance from both his sins and his enemies by the power of his victorious Lord.[8] Fidelity to Christ qualifies him for a glory which no human growth or effort could achieve.[9]

Gregory of Nyssa and Augustine have been chosen as representatives of their respective traditions. Gregory's assertion of universal salvation explicitates the tendencies of Greek thought, just as Augustine's limitation of the availability of salvation to communicants of the Catholic Church grows out of the assumptions of Latin thought and practice.

Four pairs of categories will be used in this analysis of the difference between these two theologies. A process might be continuous or discontinuous, and it might be developmental or interventionist. The graces through which God works the process of salvation might be operative or co-operative. An element in the economy of salvation might be constitutive or normative. I shall define the first two pairs and then use them to clarify the distinction between the types of grace. The remaining terms, constitutive-normative, are understood according to Peter Schineller's definitions.[10]

A continuous process involves a series of stages in which prior states are causes or conditions for subsequent ones. In a discontinuous process the prior states are not so required. Thus certain stages may be omitted in a discontinuous process but not in a continuous one. In a developmental process the prior stages are among the efficient causes of the subsequent perfections. The causal relation between its stages makes such a process continuous. Thus, the growth of the soul in acquired knowledge or virtue is a continuous, developmental process. In an interventionist process a cause external to the subject of the process produces the subsequent stage without the active co-operation of the subject and its earlier perfections. Such a process may be discontinuous, but it will be continuous if an earlier stage of the process is a condition for

---

[7] *Life of Antony* 66.

[8] Thus, the vision of the glorious Cyprian reassures the martyr in the *Acts of Montanus and Lucius* 21. See also Cyprian's *Ep.* 58.

[9] The Greek tradition thinks in terms of the cleansing and development of the soul, while the Latins use the resurrection of the body as their paradigm.

[10] See "A Spectrum of Christologies and Ecclesiologies" in Schineller above.

the external agent's operation. The resurrection of the flesh is a discontinuous, interventionist process. The granting of forgiveness to a repentant sinner and the answering of a prayer are continuous, interventionist processes. As I have noted, the Greek tradition grounds its theology in creation, respects the integrity and continuity of natural processes, and tends to be developmental in describing the economy of salvation. In the Latin tradition, however, the redemptive intervention of Christ is foundational, nature and grace are described as discontinuous, and the process of salvation is explained as interventionist but continuous.[11]

Neither Gregory's theology nor Augustine's is a pure type, since both theologians indicate the functioning of operative and co-operative graces. By operative grace I indicate a divine operation which produces its effect independently of the active participation of the human person it affects. By co-operative grace I indicate a divine operation which attains its effect by the active productivity of both divine and human agents. Thus, the created person is among the efficient causes of the effects of co-operative grace, but is not such a cause of the effects of operative grace. An operative grace may precede and cause the human efforts with which it then becomes co-operative.[12] A developmental process requires and admits only co-operative graces. An interventionist process requires operative graces. The two processes, of course, may be sequenced in a hybrid. Thus, a divine intervention may cause the human co-operation in a developmental process which then satisfies the condition for a subsequent operative grace. Gregory and Augustine use both kinds of grace to define such mixed processes in explaining the economy of salvation.

My procedure will be to examine the functioning of the economy of salvation as explained by Gregory of Nyssa and Augustine. Then I shall reflect on the relevance of patristic theologies for the work of contemporary ecclesiology.

GREGORY OF NYSSA

The assertion that salvation will be universally accomplished is based on Gregory's belief that the entire human race is the divine image in the creation. God intends a definite number of humans to be generated so that humanity itself will reach its proper perfection. Once this full

[11] This distinction between the God-creation-centered Greek tradition and the Christ-redemption-centered Latin tradition parallels the definition of the second and third of Schineller's types.

[12] In *De grat. et lib. arb.* 17, 33, Augustine describes a single grace which causes human willing and then co-operates with it in producing good works.

complement is reached, the generative process will cease and every individual will be brought to perfection. The role of humanity as the divine image requires the salvation of each and every individual.[13]

Creation and Fall

Because of his notion of the final state of humanity, Gregory distinguishes two divine intentions in its original formation. God first intends the divine image in the race as a whole and in each human person. Secondly, foreknowing the fall, in which this image will be mixed with evil, God differentiates humans sexually to provide the means of carnal generation whereby the full number of humans will be produced. Gregory seems to have thought that numerical increase would have occurred by nonsexual means had sin not entered the human race. These two phases of creation are not successive in execution. Rather, the distinction and sequence of divine intentions is used to account for the absence of sexual differentiation in the perfect state of humanity.[14]

Through this sexual differentiation, which remains extrinsic to the divine image in human persons, a way is opened for the dominance of the passions, the principal fault of fallen humanity.[15] Passions and emotions are not evil in themselves; rather, these forces and energies are good and useful when directed by reason.[16] Even in their subordinate role, however, Gregory associates the passions with the fallen state of humanity and excludes them from its final perfection.[17]

The fall of humanity goes undescribed, though its causes and consequences are carefully specified. Sin was an inevitable consequence neither of creation in the image of the divine freedom nor of sexual differentiation. The voluntary failure of Adam and Eve mingled evil in the human will and upset the balance between the energies of the soul and the passions of the body.[18] After the fall, the passions dominate the mind and direct reason to sensual satisfactions.[19] Once they rule the soul, the passions become vices.[20] They lead the person into illusion and desire for earthly things.[21] They mar the divine image by overlaying it with

---

[13] *De opif. hom.* 16, 22 (*PG* 44, 184B–D, 204C–205A); *De anim. et res.* (*PG* 46, 128BC); *De vita Moys.* (*Gregorii Nysseni opera* 7/1, 57.8–12, Jaeger edition, hereafter indicated by *GNO*).

[14] *De opif. hom.* 16, 17 (*PG* 44, 184A, 189CD).

[15] *De opif. hom.* 18 (*PG* 44, 192A–C); *Orat. cat.* 16 (*PG* 45, 49D).

[16] *De opif. hom.* 18 (*PG* 44, 193BC); *De anim. et res.* (*PG* 61A–D, 65C–68A).

[17] *De anim. et res.* (*PG* 46, 53C–56A, 89C–92A).

[18] *Orat. cat.* (*PG* 45, 29C); *De orat. dom.* 4 (*PG* 44, 1161D–1164A).

[19] *De opif. hom.* 14 (*PG* 44, 173D–176A).

[20] *Ibid.* 18 (*PG* 44, 192C–193A); *De beat.* 3 (*PG* 44, 1223BC).

[21] *De inst. christ.* (*GNO* 8/1, 40.11–41.2).

corruption.[22] Their disorder is communicated in humanity by the process of generation.[23]

Purification

Salvation involves a double process of purification and growth. The growth of the soul in knowledge and love of God is grounded in the creation of the human person in the image of God. Rather than being originally gifted with a static state of perfection, humanity was created to advance unceasingly in union with the infinite God. Because of the fall, however, a purification from passion and vice must precede and prepare for the spiritual development. The cleansing of the body from passion and of the soul from vice are distinct processes which shall be considered in turn.

Physical death can be considered a consequence of sin, but it functions as a means of salvation. In the fall, the human body was mixed with evil by the breaking out of its passions. As composed of elements, however, the flesh can be dissolved into its constituents and then reconstituted in its original purity. Gregory uses the analogy of a clay pot in which some metal has hardened. The vessel is broken away from the metal and the clay made into a paste from which the artisan reshapes the original pot. So God cleanses the polluted flesh by dissolving and forming it anew.[24] By taking humanity upon Himself, the Word of God sustained its elements through the dissolution of death and reunited body and soul inseparably. Just as the death of Adam affects all, so does the resurrection of Christ extend to all by reason of the common humanity. Christ established a process which purifies the flesh of each person who shares humanity with him.[25] This purification is completed at the end of the process of generation and death, when Christ will raise all to a new and unending life.[26]

The full purification of the body from passion is achieved in the resurrection by an operative grace, the work of Christ. The cleansing of the soul from vice, however, is by co-operative grace, which requires the effort of the human person to attain its goal. God respects the freedom which He created in human persons: sin and its purification are necessarily voluntary. The human soul must overcome its dominating

[22] De opif. hom. 18 (PG 44, 193C); De beat. 1 (PG 44, 1197B); De virg. 12 (GNO 8/1, 297.10–302.26).

[23] De beat. 6 (PG 44, 1273AB); Orat. cat. 13 (PG 45, 45A); De orat. dom. 5 (PG 44, 1184B–1185A).

[24] Orat. cat. 8, 16 (PG 45, 33A–36B, 52BC).

[25] Ibid. 16, 32 (PG 45, 52CD, 80BC); De inst. christ. (GNO 8/1, 205.22–206.9).

[26] De anim. et res. (PG 46, 148BC); De opif. hom. 17 (PG 44, 188CD).

passions and attain a state of *apatheia*, of freedom from passion, in which
the divine image is restored to serve as the foundation for a process of
growth in union with God.[27] After the resurrection, Gregory explains,
Christ will judge the state of each soul. For those whom he finds still
bound by passion and thus unable to progress in union with God, he will
prescribe a cleansing by fire.[28] Drawing the soul to good, Christ gradually
forces it to separate from evil. The process is described as torturous, but
Gregory insists that it is not punitive.[29] He does not explain its voluntary
character. The souls of infants who die before an evil life has overlaid the
divine image with corruption require no cleansing in the resurrection.[30]

   This purification of the soul may also be achieved in this world by the
voluntary asceticism of a Christian life. In baptism a person symbolically
anticipates death and resurrection in Christ and commits himself to free
his soul from vice and passion.[31] In the Eucharist Christ continues the
work of purifying the body from passion which he will complete in the
resurrection.[32] The goal of ascetical practice is purity of soul, the restoration of the divine image in the spirit.[33] Gregory cautions against a pre-
occupation with bodily exercises which would distract the soul from its
proper task.[34] One takes a stone to the soul, removes the rust and corruption from the divine image, and thereby reveals the true human voca-
tion.[35] The state of *apatheia* places one on the road of ascent to God.
Asceticism continues to free and focus the energies of the soul on the up-
ward journey to God.[36] The guidance of Christ's teaching, the inspiration
of his suffering and death, and the grace of the Holy Spirit provide the
assistance and direction necessary for this voluntary asceticism.[37]

   The process of purgation has both its operative and its co-operative
moments. An operative grace purifies the body from passion either in
death and resurrection or in the sacraments of baptism and the
Eucharist.[38] This process is interventionist and discontinuous. In contrast to this, the cleansing of the soul is described as a continuous, devel-

---

[27] *De vita Moys.* (*GNO* 7/1, 39.21–40.12, 82.17–83.22); *De orat. dom.* 4 (*PG* 44, 1168D);
De anim. et res. (*PG* 46, 160C).

   [28] *De anim. et res.* (*PG* 46, 157B–160C); *Orat. cat.* 8 (*PG* 45, 36CD).

   [29] *De anim. et res.* (*PG* 46, 97C–100C, 101B–104C).

   [30] *De infant.* (*PG* 46, 177A–181A).

   [31] *De vita Moys.* (*GNO* 7/1, 72.7–17); *Orat. cat.* 35 (*PG* 45, 85D–89C).

   [32] *Orat. cat.* 37 (*PG* 45, 93A–96B).

   [33] *De virg.* 5, 11 (*GNO* 8/1, 277.7–278.11, 294.7–295.26).

   [34] *Ibid.* 22 (*GNO* 8/1, 330.20–333.10).

   [35] *De beat.* 6 (*PG* 44, 1269B–1272B).

   [36] *Ibid.* 1, 8 (*PG* 44, 1208A–C, 1297BC); *De virg.* 8 (*GNO* 8/1, 284.21–286.8).

   [37] *De inst. christ.* (*GNO* 8/1, 41.2–9, 47.23–49.20, 53.15–54.19); *De vita Moys.* (*GNO* 7/1,
81.3–82.3, 126.11–128.13).

   [38] See nn. 31 and 32 above.

opmental process which is achieved through co-operative graces. During earthly life the human effort which complements divine grace is fully voluntary. In the cleansing by fire, however, the action of Christ produces the necessary human co-operation. The work of Christ is constitutive of the entire process of restoration of humanity to the perfection in which it was originally created.

Growth in Union with God

The second stage in the economy of salvation, spiritual growth in union with God, begins when the soul is purified and the divine image restored to prominence in it. Gregory shares the supposition of his tradition that stable and unchanging existence belongs to the divine. That which comes into being by change cannot attain or maintain a stable condition.[39] He values this change, however, as the opportunity for unlimited growth. Gregory distinguishes two forms of change, one repetitious and the other progressive.

Repetition characterizes the life of the senses. A need or desire arises and is satisfied. The satiety brings an end both to appetite and to the peculiar pleasure of satisfying it. One enjoys food and beverage, for example, only as long as hunger and thirst persist. Once satiety is reached, the satisfaction disappears and the objects of appetite become repugnant. The satiety soon passes and the desire eventually arises again. The process of sense life is compared to filling a leaky cask, which never stays full; to using a brick mold, which must be emptied as soon as it is filled; and finally to climbing a sand dune, when the size and speed of one's steps produce no advance. This form of change is simply repetitious because the limitations of sense desire exclude cumulative progress.[40]

The life of the soul, however, allows an unlimited and cumulative change which is truly progressive. The fulfilment of one goal opens the person to a fresh experience of desire rather than bringing satiety. Satisfaction whets one's appetite for still higher goals, and the pursuit of these further goods actually stabilizes the soul in those it already possesses. Gregory compares spiritual growth to a ladder or stairway in which each stage opens the way to the next one. Moreover, the freshness and increase of desire prevent the tedium associated with a homogeneous process such as Origen describes.[41] The progress of the soul is unlimited as well as cumulative. The created soul cannot stop changing, and the divine object of desire cannot be exhausted. A human soul must

[39] *Orat. cat.* 6, 21 (*PG* 45, 28D, 57D–60A).
[40] *De vita Moys.* (*GNO* 7/1, 50.3–51.5, 118.13–17); *De beat.* 4 (*PG* 44, 1244B).
[41] *De vita Moys.* (*GNO* 7/1, 112.7–113.9, 114.5–116.24); *De beat.* 2, 4 (*PG* 44, 1208D, 1245AB); Origen, *De princip.* 2, 9, 2.

eventually exhaust the limited potentialities of evil, but its growth in good can have no term.[42]

Gregory locates the proper development of humanity not in the meaningless repetition of the senses and passions but in an unlimited and ever-accelerating progress in knowledge and love of God. The mystical ascent begins when a person attains *apatheia* and discovers the image of God in his soul. The unknowable God is first perceived in this created image. Then one passes beyond all human concepts to a higher experience of the divine whose stages Gregory characterizes by a feeling of vertigo and entrance into a luminous darkness. Each stage is limited, but each opens to a higher. The process is unending, accelerating, and cumulative.[43] The ascetic may enter the way of mystical union during his earthly life once his soul is purified. Those who die as infants begin to progress in the resurrection, while those adults in whose souls the image is still obscured by passion must first be cleansed by fire.[44]

The elements of Gregory's analysis of spiritual growth, the infinite divine nature and its image in the soul, belong to the original order of creation, which is restored by the work of Christ. The process is continuous, developmental, and achieved by co-operative graces. The work of Christ seems to be limited to the purification of humanity in preparation for its growth into union with God.

Christ and the Church

The role of Christ and the Church in the process of salvation can now be specified. Christ's primary influence appears to be in the purification of the body and soul, which opens the way to growth in knowledge and love of God. Christ accomplishes the purification of the body by an operative grace through his death and resurrection. Without the restoration of the original harmony of the human person, the soul cannot grow. Christ's grace has a major role in the voluntary cleansing of the soul. No one undertakes or successfully completes a program of asceticism apart from the operative grace of baptism and the Eucharist and the co-operative grace of Christ's teaching. Further, Christ governs and directs the cleansing by fire through an operation which causes human co-operation. Finally, Christ breaks Satan's power over sinners. He alone destroys the dominion of evil and sets all persons free.[45] Thus Christ establishes the order in which human efforts can be efficacious.

[42] *De vita Moys.* (*GNO* 7/1, 3.12–4.18, 116.21–23); *De opif. hom.* 21 (*PG* 44, 201BC); *De inst. christ.* (*GNO* 8/1, 213.17–214.6).

[43] *De vita Moys.* (*GNO* 7/1, 83.23–84.20, 86.11–88.12, 89.10–14); *De beat.* 6 (*PG* 44, 1264B–1265A, 1268B–1269A).

[44] *De beat.* 6 (*PG* 44, 1273AB); *De infant.* (*PG* 46, 177A–180D).

[45] *Orat. cat.* 22, 23 (*PG* 45, 60C–64B).

Gregory does not describe a role for Christ in the process of growth in union with God. He does specify his general theory of co-operation between divine grace and human efforts by asserting that the Holy Spirit sustains the growth of the soul in knowledge of God.[46]

The emphasis on universal resurrection and subsequent cleansing by fire excludes an assertion that the Church is a constitutive element of the general process of salvation. Still, only those adults who die and rise in baptism and live its commitment to asceticism anticipate the process of purification and gain access to knowledge and love of God in this life. Because of the nature of the fall, in which the passions lead the mind into error and direct the soul's energies to sensual satisfactions, the teaching and exemplary roles of Christ, which are mediated by the Church, have a major significance. Unless a person grasps the true perfection of humanity through the intervention of Christ, he simply will not direct his ascetical efforts properly and will not attend to the divine image in his soul. Without Christ's initial cleansing of the flesh in baptism and guiding of the efforts of the soul, which are both mediated by the Church, a person either continues to satisfy the repetitious demands of the passions or becomes mired in a fruitless campaign to deny and destroy sensual life altogether.[47]

Because the Church is the sole mediator of the grace of Christ to humans during their earthly life, it is a constitutive element in this limited functioning of the economy of salvation. Moreover, precisely as anticipating the general purification which will be accomplished by death and fire, the Church has a normative role as well. Those saved during this life reach purification in the Church; those saved in the next life repeat the pattern set in the Church.

Conclusion

Gregory's explanation of the salvation of all human beings may be analyzed in the categories of continuity and discontinuity, development and intervention. He emphasizes the continuity of the entire process by setting the purification of body and soul as a foundational condition for growth in union with God. The purification of the body is through a discontinuous process, constituted by the operative intervention of Christ. The cleansing of the soul, however, is described as a continuous, developmental process in which the co-operative grace of Christ is constitutive. Finally, the growth of the soul in union with God is a continuous developmental process in which some assistance of the Holy Spirit co-operates with human desires.

[46] *De inst. christ.* (*GNO* 8/1, 45.18–47.22, 53.15–54.19); *De orat. dom.* 4 (*PG* 44, 1165A).
[47] *De vita Moys.* (*GNO* 7/1, 83.7–22); *De inst. christ.* (*GNO* 8/1, 41.2–9, 47.23–49.20); *De virg.* 22 (*GNO* 8/1, 330.20–333.10).

The economy of spiritual growth into union with God was established in creation. Christ appears to be neither constitutive nor normative in this order. Instead, his work constitutes an economy of purification through which the original order is restored after the fall. His grace operates in the purification of the body and co-operates in the cleansing of the soul. In the cleansing by fire, he causes human co-operation with his grace.

Gregory does not assign the Church a constitutive role in either the establishment or the operation of the universal economy of purification and growth. The Church does have a constitutive position in the functioning of the economy of purification on earth, because it is the sole mediator of the graces of this economy. It has a normative role in the universal economy of purification, since its life indicates the way of cleansing in the *eschaton*. Like Christ, the Church appears to have neither a constitutive nor a normative role in the economy of growth in union with God.

AUGUSTINE OF HIPPO

Augustine's writings of the period immediately after his conversion betray a perspective on creation and salvation not unlike that of the Greek tradition found in Gregory of Nyssa. While admitting certain debilitating consequences of the fall of humanity, notably mortality, he emphasizes the residual capacity of the human spirit to overcome the obstacles placed in its way by the infirmity of the flesh and to attain a certain peace in this life and beatitude in the next.[48] As he was integrated into the African Church and began to study the Pauline writings more closely, Augustine's thought took on the characteristics peculiar to the Latin tradition. These include an emphasis on discontinuity and divine intervention and the assumption that salvation is available only through the faith and sacraments of the Church.[49]

Foundations of Particularism

The Greek tradition grounds the economy of salvation in the divine creative will and explains the role of Christ as a restorer of the original order. Latin theology, however, begins with the salvific events of the life of Christ and constructs an explanation of creation and fall on the foundational assertion that Christ is the sole Savior. The schismatics in Rome and Africa and their Catholic counterparts in the third and fourth centuries insisted that salvation could be attained only through baptism

[48] This attitude is manifest in *De lib. arb.* 1 and in *De vera relig.*
[49] Augustine commented on Paul about 394–96. The new attitude begins to appear in *De lib. arb.* 3 and is clearest in *Ad Simpl.* 1.

and membership in the true communion of Christ.[50] Martin of Tours, according to the report of Sulpicius Severus, raised a catechumen from the dead and received his report of the judgment and condemnation awaiting the unbaptized.[51] Cyprian refused to recognize the martyrdom of Christians who had separated themselves from the Catholic communion.[52] Baptism and proper communion were thought absolutely necessary for salvation.

Augustine assumed the prejudices of Latin Christianity and worked them into a coherent whole which became the foundation for subsequent Western theology. He assigned a double function to Christ: he liberates from the guilt of sin, and he gives the Holy Spirit, whose charity enables a person to do the works of justice. The historical life, death, and resurrection of Jesus Christ are the foundation of the economy of salvation.[53] Moreover, the human mediation which brings a person into contact with these events in faith and the sacraments is also a constitutive element of the economy. To attain the forgiveness of sins, one must believe and be baptized in the death and resurrection of Christ.[54] To receive and retain the Holy Spirit, one must adhere to the Catholic communion.[55]

These exclusivist claims for Christ and the Church create a tension between creation and salvation. Augustine uses the doctrine of an original guilt transmitted from Adam to justify the eternal condemnation of those who have no opportunity to be joined to Christ in faith and baptism.[56] He asserts the moral impotence of human nature in order to establish that outside the sphere of the influence of the Holy Spirit no good or meritorious action can be performed.[57] Without the help available only from Christ through the Church, human persons cannot avoid sin and condemnation.

[50] Thus, Tertullian in *De pudicitia* 21, 22; Hippolytus in *Philosophumena* 9, 8; Cyprian in *Ep.* 4, 4 and *Ep.* 36, 2. The Novatianists and Donatists insisted that their converts be rebaptized, thus denying all salvific power to the rival communion.

[51] *Life of Martin* 7. In contrast, a story from the Greek tradition about Macarius' raising a man from death shows no interest in his lack of baptism; he is sent back to sleep until Christ comes. See Cassian, *Conferences* 15, 3.

[52] *Ep.* 60, 4.

[53] This is the major point of Augustine's controversy with Pelagius. See *De pecc. mer.* 3, 4, 7; *De nat. et grat.* 39, 46.

[54] *Conf.* 5, 9, 16; *De pecc. mer.* 2, 29, 47; *De pecc. orig.* 24, 28; 25, 29.

[55] This is said of Cornelius in *De bapt.* 1, 8, 10; see also *De bapt.* 3, 16, 21; *C. litt. Pet.* 2, 77, 172; *Ep.* 185, 9, 42, and 10, 46.

[56] *De nat. et grat.* 2, 2; 4, 4; 8, 9; 9, 10; *De pecc. mer.* 1, 28, 55–56; 3, 4, 7–8; *De pecc. orig.* 24, 28; 26, 31; 29, 34.

[57] Explicitly in *De nat. et grat.* 39, 46. Actually, the theory of anonymous Christianity accepts this premise but asserts that good works do occur outside the Church. This, in turn, grounds the assertion of the universal operation of the Holy Spirit.

Fall and Redemption

God originally created human persons in His image, with the capacity to discern and prefer the good.[58] Had Adam and Eve submitted to the divine command, the predetermined fulness of humanity would have been attained through sexual, though dispassionate, generation.[59] Instead, the first humans loved their created perfection more than the divine goodness and sinned in pride and disobedience. They subjected themselves and the whole of humanity in them to condemnation and to the dominion of Satan. Consequently, all their offspring are born guilty of sin and condemned to eternal punishment.[60]

God decided to rescue the number of humans necessary to fill up the places in heaven vacated by the fall of the angels.[61] To accomplish this, Augustine explains, God had to free his chosen ones from the power of these fallen angels. Humanity had freely subjected itself to Satan by sinning. Instead of destroying this evil dominion by an act of power, God arranged for Satan to overstep the bounds of his "right." Because he was born and lived without sin, Christ was not subject to the dominion which Satan exercises through death. Thus, in attacking and killing the innocent Christ, Satan exceeded the limits of his domain. By submitting to an undeserved death, Christ gained a right over Satan: he frees from sin and bondage all those united to him by faith in his victorious death and rising. Belief in Christ, therefore, brings the forgiveness of sins. Those who are not so united to Christ are held by Satan in eternal death.[62] Thus even the saints of the Old Testament were saved only through faith in the prophetic announcements of the life and death of Christ.[63]

Salvation in Christ

Faith in Christ earns the believer not only the forgiveness of sins but also the gift of the Holy Spirit, the charity by which one loves God for His own sake and delights in His commandments. Augustine establishes the necessity of this charity by three different arguments. The concupiscence of the flesh which follows upon the punishment for original sin can be restrained and overcome only if one loves the commanded good for its own sake. In the absence of such delight, one simply will not persevere in resisting carnal pleasure.[64] Next, he argues that unless one chooses the

---

[58] *De corrept. et grat.* 11, 31–12, 38; *De civ. Dei* 14, 11.

[59] *De civ. Dei* 14, 10; *De pecc. orig.* 30, 40.

[60] *De pecc. mer.* 3, 7, 14; *De pecc. orig.* 38, 43; *De corrept. et grat.* 10, 28.

[61] *De civ. Dei* 22, 1.

[62] The principal exposition of the theory of redemption is in *De trin.* 13, 10–15.

[63] *De bapt.* 1, 15, 24; *De civ. Dei* 10, 25. Augustine recognizes no anonymous salvation.

[64] This argument begins in *Propp. ex ep. ad Rom.* 40, 2; *Exp. ep. ad Gal.* 46, 4–5. It is present in *De pecc. mer.* 2, 17, 26; *De grat. Chr.* 26, 27.

good for its own sake, the willing is not truly good. The person who only seeks to avoid punishment actually prefers evil and would do it if he could escape God's justice. Charity, therefore, is necessary not only to insure performance but also to make it truly good.[65] Finally, he asserts that human nature, even in its original state, can actually choose and perform the good only with the assistance of divine grace.[66] God endowed humanity with a desire for good and even with a power to choose it. The exercise of this capacity must, however, be attributed to the divine mercy rather than to human autonomy. Augustine insists that the human person may not claim for himself the perfecting of the original divine gift.[67] The created person actually wills and performs just works only under the influence of the Holy Spirit.

Augustine explains the way in which individuals are liberated from condemnation and brought to eternal life within this framework. In his natal state, a child of Adam follows the desires of the flesh and adds personal sins to the guilt he has inherited. The enlightenment of his reason or the revelation of the law clarifies the divine command to live justly and makes him aware of his sinfulness and of the condemnation threatening him. To such an individual the gospel of Jesus Christ offers the forgiveness of sins and the assistance of the Holy Spirit for fulfilling the precepts of the law. The act of faith joins a person to Christ and frees him from guilt and the dominion of Satan. It also merits the grace of the Spirit whereby one loves God and neighbor. By giving delight in justice, charity also strengthens the will to do the works of the law. Good works, then, earn the reward of eternal glory. By faith one merits charity, and by living in charity he merits eternal life.[68]

Mediation of the Church

The Church has a constitutive role in both faith and charity. The faith which Augustine describes responds to the Church's preaching of the gospel. Only those who are reborn of water and the Spirit can enter the kingdom of God.[69] Finally, charity can be received and maintained only in the communion of the Church.

In his controversial writings against the Donatists, Augustine established membership in the Catholic communion as a condition for the indwelling of the Holy Spirit in charity and for the forgiveness of sins.

---

[65] De spir. et litt. 8, 13; 14, 26; 32, 55; De nat. et grat. 57, 67.

[66] De nat. et grat. 26, 29; 48, 56; De gest. Pel. 3, 7; Ep. 186, 10, 35 and 11, 37; De civ. Dei 14, 27.

[67] De nat. et grat. 60, 70; De spir. et litt. 7, 11; De pecc. mer. 2, 18, 30; De grat. Chr. 26, 27.

[68] See De div. quaest. 66; Propp. ex ep. ad Rom. 12; De spir. et litt. 30, 52.

[69] As early as Ad Simpl. 1, 2, 2, Augustine asserted that Cornelius needed baptism to make his faith salvific.

The Holy Spirit gives both love of God and the inseparable love of neighbor. The bond of peace in the unity of the Christian community manifests His presence and action. Consequently, Augustine argues, anyone who rejects the love of this communion and goes into schism violates charity and abandons the Holy Spirit.[70] The schismatic may believe in Christ and follow the commandments, but none of his works are good and salvific without the grace of the Spirit.[71] In the words of Christ, moreover, the reception of the Holy Spirit gives the power to forgive sins. Hence only the loving communion in which the Spirit dwells has the power to forgive sins. Its charity covers and forgives the sins of all those who adhere to it.[72] Although a person may receive baptism outside the Church, the forgiveness and charity of the sacrament are received and retained only within the Catholic communion.[73]

Augustine assigns the Church a type of constitutive role in the economy of salvation which is foreign to the Greek tradition. The Christian community not only mediates forgiveness and charity through preaching and the sacraments, but is itself a community of salvation in which the Spirit dwells.[74] Although neither faith and baptism nor Church membership are sufficient for salvation, they are constitutive of the economy in which a person receives the forgiveness and retains the charity which qualify him for God's beatifying intervention.

Conclusion

In explaining the economy of salvation, Augustine describes a process which is both continuous and discontinuous, developmental and interventionist. In its natal state, humanity seeks only sinful actions and lacks all resources to initiate the process of salvation. The divine intervention which terrifies by imposing the law constitutes the first discontinuity.[75] Thereafter, a continuous series of divine operations and human co-operative responses establishes a person in a state of salvation. When the person is properly terrified, God intervenes a second time in the preaching of the gospel and gives the operative grace of faith. The faithful person prays for charity, and the Holy Spirit is sent into his heart. This operative grace, which makes a person good, then co-operates in his good works and his prayer for perseverance.[76] God again intervenes with an operative grace to maintain His elect in innocence and love until

---

[70] *De bapt.* 1, 8, 10; 1, 9, 12; 3, 16, 21; 5, 4, 4; 5, 23, 33; *C. litt. Pet.* 2, 32, 74; 2, 77, 172; *Ep.* 185, 9, 42, and 10, 46.

[71] *De bapt.* 1, 9 12; 3, 16, 21; 4, 17, 24.

[72] *Ibid.* 3, 17, 22; 3, 18, 23; 5, 21, 29; 6, 3, 5; 6, 4, 6; 6, 14, 23; *C. Cresc.* 2, 13, 16; 4, 11, 13.

[73] *De bapt.* 1, 5, 7; 1, 14, 22; *C. Cresc.* 2, 13, 16; 2, 19, 19.

[74] Gregory recognized the mediatory role of the Church but did not describe the community as the place of encounter with the saving grace of the Holy Spirit.

[75] *Propp. ex ep. ad Rom.* 12.

[76] *Ep.* 186, 2, 4—3, 10; *Ep.* 194, 4, 16–18; *De grat. et lib. arb.* 17, 33.

death.[77] Finally, an operative grace raises and transforms the flesh and bestows on the soul the fulness of charity in the vision of God.[78]

Although Augustine insists on divine interventions which give love, faith, charity, perseverance, and beatitude, he describes the subsequent processes of seeking liberation, praying for the Spirit, and growing in charity as co-operative and developmental. Moreover, the process is continuous, because each divine gift and human response prepares for the subsequent divine intervention. The merit-reward connection expresses the continuity between the stages in the process.

Discontinuity is marked at two points, the first intervention in law and gospel and the penultimate gift of perseverance. No one, Augustine asserts, merits the divine grace which moves him to pray for charity. Nor can any good works merit the grace of perseverance which prevents a lapse into sin. A person can grow in charity but cannot stabilize himself in it. One notices, moreover, that the divine operations cause and sustain all subsequent human co-operation. Augustine uses the salvation of dying infants through the operative grace of baptism as paradigmatic of the divine sovereignty over human freedom in the process of salvation.[79] Thus he excludes all grounds for human glory and gives all praise to God.[80] These two discontinuities and the role of operative grace in Augustine's economy of salvation force the developmental aspects of the process into a marginal and even dispensable role.

Developmental continuity is central not to the salvation of individuals but to the elaboration of the City of God. This company of elect angelic and human persons has had members in every age since the creation.[81] In the time between the resurrection and coming of Christ, the society of the saints within the Catholic communion constitutes the earthly part of this City, the kingdom of God on earth. Since the saints are the place where the Spirit dwells in the Church, they communicate both the forgiveness of sins and the unitive charity to those joining their communion.[82] Thus the City of God is a cause of its own growth by mediating the grace of the Spirit. The charity which unites the saints on earth to the angels and the blessed in heaven establishes the continuity of the City of God into the *eschaton*.

The society of saints is the nucleus of the Catholic communion. Both as establishing the kingdom of God on earth and as mediating the grace

[77] *De grat. et lib. arb.* 6, 13.

[78] *De spir. et litt.* 36, 64; *De nat. et grat.* 38, 45; *De perf. just. hom.* 6, 14.

[79] *De gest. Pel.* 2, 4; *Ep.* 194, 7, 31; *De grat. et lib. arb.* 23, 45; *De corrept. et grat.* 8, 18.

[80] *Ep.* 194, 5, 19; *C. epp. Pel.* 2, 10, 23. The discontinuity of the process of salvation is designed to protect the absolute gratuity of grace which Augustine grounds on the text of Rom 9:16. See *Ad Simpl.* 1, 2, 12–13; *De grat. et lib. arb.* 7, 16.

[81] *De civ. Dei* 10, 7, 32; 10, 12, 1; 10, 19, 7.

[82] *De bapt.* 5, 27, 38; 6, 3, 5–5, 7; *C. litt. Pet.* 2, 108, 247; *C. Cresc.* 2, 21, 26.

of the Holy Spirit, this society makes the Church a constitutive element in the economy of salvation. The position of the Church is derivative from that of Christ, whose grace it dispenses. Christ alone has the right to liberate the descendants of Adam from eternal condemnation. He alone sends the Holy Spirit, who gives the love of God and neighbor. Christ and his saints are united not in their common humanity but in the bond of the Spirit's charity. The Church is the Body of Christ.[83]

REFLECTIONS

A number of significantly different suppositions distinguish the systems of Gregory of Nyssa and Augustine from the problematic of contemporary Christian theology. Each of the Fathers valued this world primarily as a means to overcome the effects of sin and to attain an otherworldly beatitude. Without denying that the fulness of humanity transcends the limitations of corporeal existence, contemporary Christian theology attempts to understand that perfection which is proper to earthly life. The process of history has been given a significance which is foreign to the perspectives of Gregory, Augustine, and the pre-Enlightenment world in general.

Secondly, on the basis of his understanding of the Creator's purpose, Gregory asserts that all human and angelic persons will be saved. On the basis of his understanding of the Savior's role, Augustine denies that all can be saved. Most contemporary theologians deny Augustine's conclusion without asserting Gregory's. Rather, they affirm that salvation is universally available and that all human persons have the opportunity to be saved.[84]

Thirdly, Gregory and Augustine assumed that certain individuals and groups occupy a privileged position in the economy of salvation. They agree that only Christians have the opportunity for salvation in this world, although Gregory asserted universal salvation in the *eschaton*.[85] Many contemporary theologians find such privilege and divine election incompatible with divine justice and assert an egalitarian economy in which salvation is both universally and equally available to all.[86]

Finally, Gregory and Augustine elaborated detailed explanations of the functioning of the economy of salvation. Because they had to account for the success of a restricted group—Christians—and because they did not

---

[83] Gregory developed no such communitarian model of the economy of salvation.

[84] This group would include such diverse theologians as Karl Barth and Karl Rahner.

[85] Gregory offered various explanations for the delay and limited extent of Christianity: *Orat. cat.* 29–32 (*PG* 45, 73D–84A). In the Pelagian controversy Augustine finally faced this question and decided for divine election: *De nat. et grat.* 4, 4.

[86] This assumption is most clearly expressed in the fourth of Schineller's types, though it can operate in the thought of those who hold the second and third types as well.

recognize subjective salvific acts without their public and explicitly Christian forms such as the hearing of the gospel, the reception of the sacraments, the practice of asceticism, and the performance of commanded works, they could offer definite expositions of the way a person reaches beatitude. Contemporary theologians must deal with an economy which reaches to all human persons and involves an unlimited variety of mediations and expressions of saving grace. They must attempt to explain how the subjective aspects of salvation can be mediated in different religious and secular structures. Their properly theological definitions of salvific self-transcendence are informed by the major symbols in which the Fathers specified the functioning of the economy, but involve neither the explicitly Christian forms nor the public verifiability which Gregory and Augustine defined.[87]

Despite the differences in suppositions and concerns of patristic and contemporary theology, the economies of salvation developed in the Greek and Latin traditions and presented by Gregory and Augustine are relevant for judging modern soteriological and historical assumptions and for elaborating a contemporary ecclesiology. From these two theologies and the traditions they represent we can generalize to two types of salvation theory which have different resources and limitations. These types can be recognized in modern ecclesiology, either in their pure forms or in various combinations.[88] By working out the inner logic of these types, we shall be able to account for the failure of some approaches to understanding the nature and mission of the Church and to indicate resources for alternatives.

To facilitate the analysis of these two patristic schemas, I shall deal with the interventionist and developmental models in their pure forms, excluding foreign elements which are present in Gregory and Augustine's own theologies. For example, Gregory's use of operative grace in sacramental theology and Augustine's explanation of purgatory cannot be integrated into the explanatory schemas they adopt.[89] The generalized interventionist schema is characterized by operative grace. It admits continuity by specifying certain human actions or states as conditional or meritorious for divine intervention. The generalized developmental schema allows only co-operative graces and requires the efficacy of human efforts in every stage of the process which leads to beatitude. It

[87] These theologically defined concepts of self-transcendence must be distinguished from those grounded only in psychology. Still, contemporary theologians cannot specify such publicly verifiable conditions for salvation as Gregory and Augustine did. Even in the Fathers such objective conditions were recognized as necessary but insufficient.

[88] The Augustinian interventionist schema is so deeply imbedded in Western theology that most theologians simply assume it.

[89] See *Orat. cat.* 33–37 (*PG* 45, 84A–93C) and *De civ. Dei* 21, 24–27.

excludes both discontinuity and operative grace, even in the final transition to beatitude. Since the resurrection of the flesh involves an operative grace, the developmental schema in this pure form can describe only the spiritual aspect of the process of salvation.[90] I now proceed to universalize these schemas and to examine their adequacy to explain the general and equal availability of salvation to all human persons.

Interventionist Schema

Universalizing the interventionist schema seems to involve severing all connections between the economy of salvation and those factors which differentiate one particular form of human existence from another. If no conditions must be fulfilled to qualify for divine operation, then the process is completely discontinuous and independent of the forms of human life.[91] If continuity is asserted, then the conditions must be such that they can be fulfilled in any human situation. Moreover, the equal probability of any person's attaining beatitude excludes salvific significance from any particular form of human growth. All those factors which distinguish the life situation of one person from that of another must be irrelevant for attaining salvation. Such an egalitarian economy would restrict salvific significance to that human growth which involves only aids and means which are universally and equally available. In devaluing the particularities of human environments, this theory excludes from the economy of salvation social institutions which promote human development and cause cultural differentiation. All religious traditions, not only the Christian Church, are thus excluded from significant roles.

Further, in any interventionist schema the divine action is both necessary and sufficient to produce the full perfection of human existence regardless of the prior development of the human person. In such a schema those forms of human growth which are not relevant for the fulfilment of a condition for divine operation are deprived of ultimate religious significance. The divine action which produces the beatifying perfection of the saved person will supply any fulfilment not achieved during earthly life. Social institutions which promote the advancement of individuals and the race in the unnecessary perfections have no salvific purpose.

Human institutions could gain some effectiveness in the economy of salvation if one denied that salvation is equally available to all persons and allowed various forms of human growth to influence the fulfilling of the conditions for divine intervention. Even in this instance, however, the divine operation which completes the perfecting of each person

---

[90] In Gregory's explanation the body is purified by operative graces.

[91] This would be true of Gregory's explanation of the purification of the body through death and resurrection.

deprives his earlier achievement of a final significance. If growth within this world and final perfection are discontinuous, or if the former is only a condition for the divine operation which produces the latter, the advance of humanity can be assigned only a limited religious significance.

The interventionist model offers great resources to modern theologians. If one chooses to assert some continuity between this life and the next, it allows the specification of such conditions for divine intervention as can be achieved in any human situation. Moreover, it allows divine operation to supply for the inadequacies of human growth and the regressions of sin. Because the interventionist model involves the substitution of divine operation for human achievement, it restricts the ultimate value of human effort. When it is grounded on an assertion of the equal availability of salvation, this schema imposes severe limitations on the role of religious and other human institutions in the process of salvation.

Developmental Schema

Because of its continuity and insistence on co-operation between human efforts and divine action, the developmental model avoids the limitations of the interventionist schema. It can ground the religious significance of individual and social growth and the enterprises of human history. However, it entails inequalities in different human situations which are significant for salvation and thus involves a form of privilege and election of some individuals and groups.

In this schema human effort is effective in every stage of the process of attaining perfection. Divine grace co-operates with but never replaces human action. Thus the stages in the process are intrinsically and continuously related by the functioning of created means. As attained in such a process, beatitude will be the product of human effort and co-operative divine grace rather than of the intervention of an operative grace.

If the means of growth toward perfection are neither exclusively contained within the created nature of each person nor given only by unmediated interior graces, then the economy of salvation will include social institutions which foster religious growth. Religious traditions which inspire and guide the efforts of their adherents provide significant assistance in the process of development. If a person concentrates on a form of growth which is peripheral to the true goal of humanity, his efforts are wasted. Thus, champions of the Egyptian desert who fixed their attention on the subjection of the flesh failed to advance in spiritual union with God.[92] If the unity or continuity of nature and grace forms a part of the explanation of the economy, then all institutions which affect

[92] See nn. 30 and 47 above.

the actualization of human potential become relevant for attaining beatitude. The social institutions which constitute the cultural context of an individual's life would help his religious growth to the extent that they encourage and provide means for it. Growth would be retarded by social institutions which disvalue it or deprive the individual of appropriate means. Thus a religious motivation would ground the commitment to the evolutionary development of humanity, which increases the resources available for individual progress.[93]

Because of the significance it gives to the human environment and to the institutions which differentiate one environment from another, the developmental schema excludes the assertion that human individuals have equal opportunities in the pursuit of perfection. Any attempt to re-establish egalitarianism by special interior graces to individuals in deficient cultures would undercut the religious significance of human institutions. Actually, the imperfection of every human environment limits the inequality implied by this salvific significance of cultural institutions. In a developmental schema spiritual growth would not be limited to terrestrial life.[94] Thus one could recover some egalitarianism by a sort of eschatological affirmative-action program in which God specially assists the deprived.

Church as Normative and Constitutive

One cannot assign any religious institution a significant normative role in an egalitarian economy of salvation. In a system in which salvation is universally but not equally available, a religious tradition which can justify a claim to normative status by mediating a divine revelation of the true goal of humanity and the way to attain it would have a peculiar value. Its inspiration and guidance would provide to its adherents the best available assistance in fulfilling the conditions for divine intervention or developing toward full perfection. It could also have a significant role in fostering the proper growth of other religious traditions and secular institutions. In a universalist economy all traditions and institutions can mediate divine grace. Hence a normative church would be influenced by these other institutions but would judge according to its own normative resources.[95]

The constitutive function of the Church might be understood in two nonexclusive ways. The Church might be a necessary mediator of the

[93] This conclusion follows whether one asserts that natural development is identical with religious development, a necessary condition for it, or simply an aid to it.

[94] Gregory specifies that spiritual growth is unending.

[95] In his article on mission Roger Haight seems to argue from such a normative function of the Church.

means of salvation or the earthly form of a heavenly reality. Each must be examined in a universal economy.

To assign a constitutive function to any particular religious institution, one must specify the relation between the plurality of communities of the present age and the social unity of the *eschaton*. If the eschatological kingdom of God brings an abrupt end to all churches and replaces them with a new social unity, then no earthly institution has this constitutive role.[96] If, however, the eschatological community is achieved by the transformation of some particular church whose reality continues in the new age, then the religious unity of humanity would be anticipated in that one institution and all other communities would attain fulfilment only in being joined into it in the *eschaton*. Because this church would already contain the final unifying principle of saved humanity in which all individuals and institutions reach perfection, it would be a constitutive element in the economy of salvation. Such a constitutive function could be expressed in either a continuous interventionist or a developmental schema. Gregory concentrates on individual salvation and describes only the mediatory function of the Church, but Augustine's description of the City of God located within the Catholic communion would make that Church such a constitutive element.[97]

CONCLUSION

The theory of universally available salvation indicates a shift in perspective which distances the contemporary Christian theologian from most of his predecessors. In this context the need for a new ecclesiology is immediately and strikingly evident. The results of the present investigation of patristic theology indicate that the Church must be understood through its relations to the other elements in the economy of salvation. A theory of the nature and task of the Church rests upon certain assumptions and assertions about human perfection, the process through which it is attained, and the interaction of divine grace and human effort in this process. To build an ecclesiology adequate to the new universalism, we must elaborate a new understanding of the entire economy of salvation. The purpose of this article has been to clarify two schemas of the economy and their resources for the work of contemporary theology.

[96] Christians would still attempt to convert others to acknowledge and live the truth of the relationship of humans to God through the Church. Such a form of life would be religiously significant but would not necessarily advance an individual's salvation. Church members would have access to an explicit union with God not available to others.

[97] This appears to be Robert Sears's line of argument for the constitutive nature of the Church in his "Trinitarian Love as Ground of the Church."

IV

MISSION: THE SYMBOL FOR UNDERSTANDING THE CHURCH TODAY

ROGER D. HAIGHT, S.J.

Jesuit School of Theology in Chicago

IN ADDRESSING the question of the Church in today's world, I will present the following ideas and imperatives according to a pedagogical scheme that has been characterized by some educators as problematization. Such a procedure entails, of course, more than an arbitrary device for facilitating communication. It may be taken as fundamental to human understanding that the mind addresses data with questions, and that there can be no really critical grasp of anything unless what is to be understood responds to an active and inquiring intelligence. It seems to me, moreover, that in the question of the Church today the inquiry should be marked by a sense of urgency, because the problems faced by the Church in the modern world are many and real.

In the first part of the essay, after outlining the fundamental problem that besets the Christian looking at his Church, I will suggest that the question of the Church today is a moral one, that is, a problem of concrete decision and action. At the same time, all attempts to reduce the problem of the Church to merely one of action fail to see that the problem lies just as deeply in the domain of theological understanding. In the second part, I will enumerate some of the theological resources and developments that may be employed for dealing with the problem of the Church. In the third section, I will outline briefly how these theological data might be employed to begin to frame a consistent understanding of the Church for today's culture.

Throughout this essay the word "Church" refers to the visible Church, that is, the community which is in varying degrees and at various levels organized and institutionalized,[1] and which calls itself "church."

---

[1] The word "institution" and its derivatives are used neutrally throughout this essay to refer to the public forms, patterns, role differentiation, and discipline that are assumed by any stable community. I realize that institutions are often at odds with the spontaneity of the original "spirit" of a religious community and thus are often considered a negative factor in religion; it is assumed here that they can also be positive. The usage, moreover, is not exclusive, as if to suggest that the Church is "only" or "merely" an institution. The point is rather that we are dealing with the concrete and empirical Church of history, and as such it will always have an external and more or less objective form. Finally, since I am Roman Catholic, that particular bias will be noted, but I hope that what I say of the Church has more universal relevance.

THE CHURCH AS PROBLEM

Many and varied are the problems that face the ecclesiologist as he approaches an understanding of the Church. But one problem today seems more basic than all the rest and may be considered the fundamental problem of the Church. This problem is radical in the sense that it involves the very basis or reason for being a religious person and a Christian. Logically, only after that question receives a positive response does the question of being a member of the Church arise. This problem of the Church is also fundamental in the sense that it challenges the very right of the Church to exist. In order to answer such a question, one must arrive at the very *raison d'être* of the Church. The problem referred to can be seen from two closely related points of view, or as having two reciprocally related dimensions. These concern the immanence and transcendence of the Church.

Church Immanent?

Two suppositions underlie this dimension of the problem of the Church. The first is theological and may be expressed baldly in this way: Any Christian doctrine and consequently any understanding of the Church must enter into and correlate with human experience.[2] Christian doctrines cannot be conceived of as preformed teachings from on high, worked out coherently in themselves, and passively received by the human race. Rather, theological and doctrinal expressions of faith must express faith as it is generated in people's lives and experienced in each age and culture. So central and fundamental and, in a sense, so obvious is this principle that it may be stated somewhat categorically that unless a teaching or doctrine on the Church is experienced as meaningful and relevant for life in this world, whether it confirm, confront, or seek to transform life in this world, it is non-sense.

The second supposition resides in the cultural phenomenon that more and more human beings are experiencing a feeling of being at home in this world and of responsibility for much of the human condition. Whether naturalism, or historical consciousness and secularism, or (as some suggest) Christianity itself, or all of these together are responsible for this, does not concern us here. What is important is the growing cultural phenomenon itself. To a greater or lesser degree human beings are subjects of history, and the way we corporately exercise our freedom

---

[2] Maurice Blondel was the first to express this for Catholic theology in a systematic way, and he did so with such decisiveness that it is accepted by most theologians today. The principle should not be taken to obscure the fact that religious experience is often prophetic and that God may be experienced as Judge. It simply asserts, almost tautologically, that such judgment and authority must also be experienced in order to be relevant.

in history bears an ultimate significance, whether of positive or negative import, for ourselves and the future. However distorted by selfish concerns, however perverted by ignorance, however contradicted in actual fact by ambiguous decisions, the implicit and constant desire of men and women today is to build a better world and a more humane society for all. Thus the human quest to find meaning in the world and in history is becoming more and more a conscious one. Not even the threat of death or the general experience of finitude undermines this conviction that life in this world must make sense in this world. While we are alive, this world is our home. Of itself, the promise of an afterlife, or a world outside and beyond this world, need not be any answer at all to the question of the meaning of life in this world and of how to live it; for the question of the meaning of human history arises from within history itself, and the fact of afterlife does not answer the question of the mode of conduct which is appropriate to this life. In fact, a reliance on such an afterlife, if it is extrinsic to human history, *may* negate the values of the very history it seeks to affirm.

If these suppositions be true, then it follows that any understanding of the Church today must correlate with the experience that people have of themselves, of their world, and of the project that they envisage as possible in and for this world.[3] Moreover, if these suppositions be true, the most serious objection to any doctrine of the Church is contained in the one put forward by secular humanism, namely, that Christianity and being a member of the Church distract human beings from their project in history and rob them of their responsibility for the events of history. One can, of course, formulate retorts to the classical articulations of this charge in such thinkers as Feuerbach and Freud, Marx and Dewey, and others, but such an effort would miss both the force and the truth of their statement. Its persuasive power resides in the fact that what was once the formulation of the experience of a rather rationalistic culture of the nineteenth and early-twentieth centuries has now become the common consciousness, in varying degrees, of a large portion of generally educated persons in the world today. Throughout the world the Church has a mortal rival in either Marxism of one sort or another or in other social humanitarian movements.[4] The truth of their critique lies in its accuracy in describing what has happened in the modern period.

[3] This is a major theme in Karl Rahner's *The Shape of the Church to Come* (London, 1974).

[4] These movements and their specific appeals and promises, their particular logics and languages, vary greatly in different parts of the world. Yet they agree on certain basic suppositions about the nature of humanity and the task that is ours in this world. Both these differences and these commonalities must be appreciated if one is to see the relevance of social humanitarian movements in other parts of the world and the pertinence for one's own situation of the various Christian responses to them and adaptations from them.

A direct polemic against, or an attempted refutation of, secular humanism would also be out of place because it would beg the question; it would inevitably fail to grant the truth in the humanist critique on another level, that is, its *inner* element of truth. God, after all, is God, and as transcendent *mysterium tremendum et fascinans* has the power to draw the human person and a whole community into Himself with the absoluteness that is correlative to and inherent in an experience of God. The mystics testify that such an absorption can be total, and William James confirms that all religious experience is in some degree mystical.[5] There is, then, an essential and intrinsic tendency in religion to draw a person or a people out of this world, to devalue history, to say that our true home is not here but in heaven, and to seek forgiveness from God without attending to our neighbor whom we have hurt.[6] Christianity and the life of the churches are hardly an exception to this law.

The Church is most severely touched by the humanist critique of Christian faith because in church the dangers of religion have been institutionalized in structures and public language. The phrase "the Church and the world" is symbolic of the many categories that have functioned as dualisms, although they are not necessarily such, and thus have served to cut the Church off from history: supernatural and natural, salvation history and secular history, the sacred and the profane, eternity and time. There is a tendency to absolutize and divinize the Church itself.[7] For example, the concept of the "Body of Christ" can be and has been employed in such a way that the Church is hypostasized into a divine entity with divine qualities of authority and holiness subsisting above history. Authority and holiness are seen adhering in the institutional Church whether or not the historical criteria of these moral and theological qualities are met. To the extent that the Church today remains that institution or those communities or groups who possess the word and the sacraments as the means for the eternal salvation of their members, it is peculiarly vulnerable to the humanist critique; for this is a definition of a privileged group, set aside in history, whose self-under-

---

[5] William James, *The Varieties of Religious Experience* (New York, 1961) p. 299. This does not mean that mystical or religious experience necessarily withdraws one from the world. What is being said here is that this is an intrinsic psychological possibility and constant danger. On the other hand, one may insist that the condition for the possibility of mystical experience is the immanence of God to persons, to history, and to the world. Thus the concept one forms of God becomes vitally important. Finally, the question of holiness is raised here and will be addressed at the end of this essay.

[6] See Reinhold Niebuhr, *Moral Man and Immoral Society* (New York, 1960) pp. 51–82.

[7] See Hans Küng, *The Church* (New York, 1967) pp. 129–32, 234–41. This tendency can be seen in Augustine, especially when he stands in contrast to a thinker such as Gregory of Nyssa. See J. Patout Burns, "The Economy of Salvation in Patristic Theology," earlier in this issue.

standing revolves around its own exclusive possession of Christ and his grace.[8]

Church Transcendent?

Again, two suppositions underlie an appreciation of this dimension of the problem of the Church. The first is cultural, the second theological. Contemporary culture may be characterized as empirical-minded and critical. People today distrust every kind of abstract knowledge, especially when it is raised to the level of ideology or objectivized doctrine. One wants to know how one can be sure of this or that doctrine: "How is it known?" Here, too, the philosophies of empiricism, pragmatism, and a "scientific mentality" have filtered down to common consciousness, so that men and women in our world want proof, if they are interested at all in something. Suspicious of authority, they instinctively apply a quasi-positivistic criterion of truth—seeing, touching, experiencing. Credulity is no virtue. Aware of historical relativity and pluralism, people cannot simply accept religious doctrines on the basis of external authority. Rather, in all honesty, they challenge their proponents: "Show me!"

The second supposition is the theological one that the Church does have a divine quality and a transcendent source of its coming-to-be and continued existence in history. No Christian would deny some relation to God as underlying the existence of the Church. The Church is not merely a social institution or voluntary association alongside all others, and a sociological examination or explanation of its nature and function does not exhaust the mystery it contains and is. The Church *is* by a power and energy that comes from a ground that reaches beyond history and culture.

If these suppositions be true, taken in conjunction they indicate where and how the Church must display this transcendence. The transcendence of a Church in history and in the world, among people who live in history and in the world by historical and experiential criteria, must also be manifested in the empirical history of everyday life—that is, if it is to be perceived. The Church, one can say, exists in a twofold relationship. It is related to the world, because it is a part of this world and part of apparently secular history. It is also related to the transcendent God and is the expression of His saving love for history and the race. But these two relationships are mutually interdependent. Without a faithful contact with God, it has lost its transcendence. Conversely, in being relevant to the world, if the Church capitulates to society and culture, especially their sinful patterns of behavior, it has also lost its transcendence. "Since the Church is *in* secular culture, and all its people actually exist there,

[8] See the first type of Christology and ecclesiology in J. Peter Schineller, "A Spectrum of Christologies and Ecclesiologies," earlier in this issue.

the life of the congregation cannot in any sense express transcendence of the culture around it unless it is willing to challenge the injustice and sins of the wider community in which it lives."[9]

There is no question about the fact that the Church claims transcendence and even proclaims it. But those claims, which have been abstract and dogmatic, invite testing. Too often they have been symbolized in an isolation from the world, or a disinterest in it, and associated with sacred ceremonies performed in the corner of everyday life and on special days. The institutional witness to transcendence is mainly visible in holy places, ritual ceremony, and the uniforms of office. In terms of freedom from sin and love of neighbor, corporate Christian life on the whole appears no different from that of any other group. The saints, both past and present, appear at times to have provided us with our own cargo system. The commandment of love of neighbor, which is the touchstone of the transcendence spoken of here, has often been explicitly limited in both intention and practice to "one's own." But where that is the case, one can scarcely speak of transcendence at all.

The question of the Church outlined in its two dimensions is really one problem: the failure of the Church to become immanent to the world because of an inappropriate transcendence, and its failure to witness to transcendence precisely because of its failure at immanence.[10] The problem is the problem of the Church's credibility. In phrasing the question thus, one seems to invite the cliché that "the real problem of Christianity is that it has never been tried." If people would only live the Christian life, the truth of the Church would become self-evident. This attitude, however, fails to grasp the nature of the problem, because it does not see that what is at stake here also involves a fundamental understanding of the very nature and function of the Church. The problem is integrally religious and theological as well as moral, simply because these dimensions cannot be separated. In spite of this, there still

---

[9] Langdon Gilkey, *How the Church Can Minister to the World without Losing Itself* (New York, 1964) p. 71; cf. also p. 27.

[10] I am not saying that this failure is complete or total. And it should be noted that Christianity is able to hear the criticism of secular humanism precisely because an engagement with the world is intrinsic to Christianity. Christianity is not a gnosticism that emancipates one from history and the world. Thus, on the one hand, the criticism of humanism is in principle unjustified. But on the other, it recalls Christian responsibilities that are sometimes neglected. Finally, as to the need that the Churches listen to these criticisms, it should not be forgotten that they may stem from Christian principles, even from grace. As Tillich put it, "There are many people who are critical of the Church, Christianity, and religion generally. Many times this criticism comes from the latent Church, is directed against the manifest Church, and is often effected through the power of principles which belong to, and should be effective in, the manifest Church itself" ("Missions and World History," in Gerald H. Anderson, ed., *The Theology of the Christian Mission* [New York, 1961] p. 288).

remains the tendency to make a radical distinction between understanding the Church and observing its actual performance, or between the "real" Church and its institutional or historical form. Thus, one is inclined to say, after listening to a critical account of Church action in history, that such does not undermine the fundamental credibility of the Church.[11] But for the empirical-minded person this distinction—better, this separation—is impossible.

This ability to separate essence and existence, substance and action, reality and performance is precisely the problematic of the Church today. Granted that the Church is not primarily or simply an institution, still one cannot radically distinguish the concretely existing Church from its institutional forms. The public, social, and institutional structures of the Church deeply influence the Christian life of both the individual and the community at every level of existence. So, too, the reality of the Church and its performance cannot be neatly distinguished. After existentialism, it remains axiomatic that being, nature, substance, or essence cannot be separated from action. And the same is true for understanding or knowing. Action flows out of knowledge, and specific forms of action follow upon specific understandings. Reciprocally, one can find behind, within, and implicit to every human action, as well as the lack of it, an intentionality and a logic which either implicitly or explicitly constitute a fundamental understanding of reality. This principle must also be applied to church existence and action; a self-understanding resides there, one that is, reciprocally, constitutive of the Church as it exists today.[12] At stake, then, for Christian theology is the fundamental question of understanding and formulating the basic nature and function of the Church in the world today. This problem is not perfectly identical with that of the nature of Christianity and the Christian life, even though it is intimately related to it; for there are many Christians today—and their number is increasing—who lead lives which are exemplary personal witnesses to Christ and who are at the same time alienated from the Church and its representatives. Such people are a living response to the humanist critique. But insofar as they

---

[11] Gregory Baum, *The Credibility of the Church Today* (New York, 1968) p. 80. I do not mean to give too much weight to this isolated statement of Baum. His thesis is "that Charles Davis [*A Question of Conscience* (New York, 1967)] has described in the Catholic Church the social pathology that threatens every institution" (*ibid.*, p. 63). And, after all, he wrote this book to respond to the criticism and attempt to establish the Church's credibility.

[12] This does not imply that knowledge is virtue. One should not minimize the power of sin within the Church. The thesis states simply that the relative failure of the Church to respond to the modern exigencies of the world through action reveals its failure to respond to the challenge for a renewal of self-understanding.

lead self-transcending lives in the world, they raise the question, from within Christianity itself, why belong to a Church? The problem addressed here, then, is the problem of the Church.

Finally, in order to define the theological strategy for addressing this question, it may be said that the critique spoken to the Church by secular humanism cannot and should not be minimized; it is not a problem to be solved once for all. We have already referred to its truth quality. It is not a question to be set up and knocked down. The experiences which have generated the humanist critique lie deeply embedded in modern culture at large and hence are shared by both non-Christians and Christians alike insofar as they share this culture. The point, then, is that this criticism does not come merely from outside Christianity; the problem exists *for* Christians and *within* the Church. And insofar as the secular-humanist objection represents basic elements of the contemporary experience of both Christian and non-Christian alike, it must be incorporated into and allowed to inform one's view of the Church. What, then, are some of the theological resources that may allow this to happen?

THEOLOGICAL RESOURCES FOR ADDRESSING THE PROBLEM

What follows is neither a complete ecclesiology nor a statement of all the resources and data for framing an understanding of the Church. The purpose is not to examine carefully either Scripture or tradition, both of which are needed to ground an adequate or complete theology of the Church. The aim here is much more modest: to list some of the theological moves or shifts that are both available and necessary for beginning to understand the Church today, especially in the light of the problem which confronts it. I wish to examine the situation and experience which form the a priori context out of which an approach to the past must be made.

Concrete, Existential, Historical Viewpoint

To begin, theology today must assume (and to a large extent has assumed) a concrete, existential, and historical point of view. This statement scarcely defines a particular methodology in theology, but rather suggests an a priori stance, attitude, and approach that must underlie any theology of the Church today. Some characteristics of this attitude are collapsed into the three adjectives, which have overlapping and interrelated senses.

The word "existential" is used in opposition to an "objective" and "essentialist" mode of thought, based on the suppositions of naive realism, in which reality is considered "out there" in such a way that it can be known, manipulated, and exactly represented in concepts and language. The word "historical," as opposed to its contradictory "ahistorical," points to the realization that all understandings and ideas, even the most universal, are rooted in history, are conditioned by particular circumstances in which they are generated, and share the note of singularity and particularity of the consciousness in which they exist. The quality of thinking called "concrete" is opposed to that which is purely "abstract" and conceptual. Since abstraction is the condition of the possibility of human thought, what concrete thinking and logic seek to avoid is conceptualism. Methodologically, concrete thought is empirical (in the healthy sense of Aquinas), experiential, and phenomenological, but with the added note of being critical. A concrete, existential, and historical theology will try to understand the Church as it has and does appear in history and in the light of the data or "facts" as they appear to our consciousness. It will try to avoid the objectifying, hypostasizing, and indeed projecting tendency to view the Church as a reified idea, existing above history, but hardly corresponding with everything else one knows to be real. The Church cannot be a product of "fideism" and an object of "pure" faith.

Apologetic Theology

The over-all form for a theology of the Church today must, for several reasons, be apologetic. Apologetics has as its primary referent the common experience of mankind. Included in its audience, therefore, are both those inside the Church and outside it. It seeks to discover and explain, not to "prove" but to disclose the Church both to Christians and to those outside. In so doing, this theology must appeal to and attempt to be adequate to common human experience. This context is thrust upon us by our new and vivid consciousness of the world and its long history and of our minority status in it. After two thousand years and in a world that is predominantly non-Christian, the Church cannot *presume*, even in its own self-understanding, its absolute truth and right to exist in history with those absolute claims.[13] A second reason stems from the fact that the world,[14] now used in a different sense, is within the Church. The Church is not over against but part of the world, so that secular consciousness and ideals, the everyday desires and aspirations and

---

[13] Augustine's theology offers an extreme example of absolute claims for the visible Church, because in his thought the Church tended (although he realized the Church was sinful) to become identified with the kingdom of God on earth. See Burns, *art. cit.* This apologetic approach to the Church and the question of the Church that flows from it make up one of the distinctive features of Juan Luis Segundo's *The Community Called Church* (Maryknoll, N.Y., 1973).

[14] In the first sense the term "world" denotes the non-Christian sphere; in this second sense it refers to the empirical world with its history and culture. This usage will be explained further in a later part of my paper.

experiences of the human race, are also those of Christians. It is precisely for this reason that apologetic theology is also an essay at self-understanding.

An apologetic context for a theology of the Church means that one draws on the same resources for self-understanding as in systematic or doctrinal theology, that is, history and contemporary Christian experience. However, the context is severely altered and different. Scripture and tradition and contemporary Christian experience can no longer be analyzed, interpreted, and integrated in an isolated manner in order to form a self enclosed understanding of the Church. Such an understanding is inadequate to our total experience and risks being uncritical. Rather, just as personal self-understanding and identity definition are dialogic and achieved in the interrelation of self with others, society, and the world at large, so too the Church must be approached in its relation to the world in the sense of non-Christian history and in its being-in-the-world of the secular everyday. Thus the Church must take into account the cultural phenomena referred to earlier in order to frame an understanding adequate to contemporary experience.

The New Question of the Church

I have just suggested that the initial approach to the theological understanding of the Church should be the question "Why the Church?" [15] There is another reason why this is so. One of the presuppositions or principles that has revolutionized ecclesiological understanding is the now common one that there *is* salvation outside the Church. Not only is the doctrine "No salvation outside the Church" wrong,[16] but also, statistically speaking, the common, normal, and "ordinary" way and place of salvation is outside the Church. Up to now, and in the foreseeable future, salvation has been and will be achieved for the vast majority of people without any empirical historical connection with Jesus of Nazareth.[17]

[15] This question and the theme which follows underlie Richard P. McBrien's *Do We Need the Church?* (New York, 1969). See also his informative *Church. The Continuing Quest* (New York, 1970) and his strategy for Church reform in *The Remaking of the Church* (New York, 1973).

[16] See Schineller's first type of Christology and ecclesiology, *art. cit.* One can certainly investigate the historical genesis of the doctrine of *Nulla salus* and by interpretation find beneath it an authentic Christian experience even for our day. The problem is that these interpretations are never quite clearly communicated by the common usage of the words employed in the proposition. A further problem is that the same can usually be done for heretical doctrines of the past. For example, while the Pelagian doctrine presented by Augustine was rightly condemned, implicit within it are a legitimate concern for the value of human freedom and a view of God who makes His salvation universally available. See R. Haight, "Notes on the Pelagian Controversy," *Philippine Studies* 22 (1974) 26–48.

[17] A denial of this position, it seems, would equally involve a denial of the predominant efficacy of God's universal salvific will and the power of His grace.

This represents a dramatically new common Christian consciousness. It does not mean that most major theologians of the past denied the possibility of salvation outside the Church. For example, they all made accommodations for Abraham, the prophets, and in general the saints of the Old Testament, if not even for the *puer in silvis*. But they had to go to extraordinary lengths to do so, because the history of theology in the West posits a very close relationship between explicit revelation and redemption, between explicit faith and grace. But whereas in the past these were most often considered, practically speaking, coextensive, it is commonly held today that they are not mutually determinative. If this be so, then the following thesis seems unassailable: When one passes from a common presupposition that there is no salvation outside the Church to the supposition that indeed the "ordinary" way of salvation is outside the Church, one must also pass to a fundamentally different understanding of the nature and role of the Church.[18]

The effects of this turn can be seen as twofold. First, the Church is "uncentered" in the world, and even in salvation history. The working of God's saving grace in all of history is maximized; the necessity and importance of the Church is perforce lessened.[19] Rather than being the center, the "kingdom of God" or the "reign of God" in all of history supplants the Church as center, and the Church becomes relative to or related to the wider and broader workings of God's grace in the world, in religious as well as "secular" history.

Second, in this context once again the first fundamental question concerning the Church is altered, this time on the grounds of Christian revelation itself.[20] The question can no longer be "What is the Church?" on the supposition the Church has an unquestioned necessity in history as the guarantor of ultimate salvation. Rather, the question concerning the Church again appears as "Why the Church?" The paradoxical but real question of the Christian who asks "Why be a Christian?" on the ground of a Christian revelation of the universal acceptance of history by

[18] See Schineller, *art. cit.*

[19] The necessity and importance of the Church is lessened relative to the final salvation of individuals and groups of people. The point here is to analyze the shift of consciousness that has occurred and its consequences. From another point of view one may say that because of its minority status the importance of the Church is heightened.

[20] Christianity has commonly held the universal salvific will of God to be a central element of revelation. This objective will of God only becomes objective reality insofar as every human individual is actually affected by the offer of saving grace. In the words of Karl Rahner, "It is part of the Catholic statement of Faith that the supernatural saving purpose of God extends to all men in all ages and places in history. . . . Because of God's universal saving purpose, the offer and possibility of salvation extends as far as extends the history of human freedom" ("History of the World and Salvation-History," *Theological Investigations* 5 [Baltimore, 1966] 103).

God and the universal possibility of salvation becomes the Church's own question. Because it is radical and critical, "Why the Church?" is the only question which will yield an answer that will suffice for Christian understanding today.[21]

Functional Answer

If it is true that the question of the Church has shifted from "What is the Church?" to "Why the Church?" then too the answer concerning the Church will change. I suggest that the new question leads almost inevitably, though often imperceptibly, to a functional answer. One answers the question "What is the Church?" substantively. Such a question asks after the nature of this more or less institutionalized voluntary organization: the Church is the "Body of Christ," the community of faith and sacraments, the hypostasized or personified "Bride of Christ." But one answers the question "Why the Church?" functionally: the purpose of the Church is to do this, or the role of the Church is to accomplish that.

These two understandings of the Church are not exclusive; this will be shown below. However, they are two fundamentally different ways of approaching an understanding of the Church.[22] The first leads to an understanding of the Church as a "thing-in-itself" or an independent society or community. For example, a substantive view of the Church may look at the Church "primarily in terms of its societal or institutional endowments," and see that substance of the Church as having existed from the beginning in one particular historical and visible community.[23] The second understanding is generated out of the relational context of the apologetic question itself and sees the Church as a community

---

[21] This shift can also be seen in the growing importance of the theme "the Church and the world." The status of this question is slowly passing from a corollary or related topic in ecclesiology to a central issue; what was formally a special question is now being perceived as the heart of the matter. It is in this sense that the term "radical" is used in this paper; no political biases are intended.

[22] These two understandings do not necessarily exclude each other; for while the substantive question can be answered without clear reference to the function or purpose of the Church, the inverse is not the case: language about the purpose and function of the Church necessarily presupposes and includes what one is talking about. Therefore, in any contrast between these two approaches to the Church, it should not be imagined that the question "Why the Church?" generates a "merely functional" or only a descriptive sociological understanding of what the Church does or should be doing in the world. It will be shown below how the function of the Church includes a conception of its "substance."

[23] Avery Dulles, "The Church, the Churches, and the Catholic Church," THEOLOGICAL STUDIES 33 (1972) 209, 200-203. Such an institutional definition of the Church is not exhaustive of possible substantive views. Sears, e.g., defines the Church substantively as a community; see his article "Trinitarian Love as the Ground of the Church" later in this issue.

intrinsically in relation to the world, to the secular, non-Christian sphere. From the very question of the role of the Church in the world it appears that the Church is not *simply* constituted by a "vertical" relation to God through the risen Christ, but also by a purposeful or intentional relation to non-Church in the world. Such a view of the Church will consequently be "relative," [24] one in which the Church will be seen as essentially influenced by the particular world it is addressing and affected by it. Such an a priori will generate an ecclesiology considerably different from one whose goal is to establish universal and normative institutional structures, or one which defines the Church simply as community. In this view, essential structures will primarily be grasped "empirically," as it were, in their constancy in and through history and in accordance with the specific task or service they are meant to accomplish.[25]

Again, a substantive approach to the Church will first determine the nature of the Church and, in light of this, decide what it can do in the world according to its predetermined nature. In this sense, and in terms of the overworked but still useful adjectives "static" and "dynamic," a substantive understanding is static. A relational and functional under-standing of the Church will be dynamic in the sense that it will involve decisions concerning what the Church is supposed to be doing in the world and interpret and adjust the institutions accordingly.

With those methodological considerations in view, we must now address the issue of the theological resources for responding to the functional question of "Why the Church?" in more specific terms.

Mission Theology

One does not have to look hard to find a scriptural and traditional symbol responding to the question of the dynamic and functional relation of the Church to the world. The symbol is "mission." Mission theology is the one locus in ecclesiology that answers directly the functional question of the Church in the wider world context. Though formerly no more than a footnote to the study of the Church, in the last seventy-five years the study of the mission of the Church has become a discipline in itself. Moreover, the theology of the mission of the Church has shown a remarkable development over these years, and has mediated

---

[24] This is to say "relative to the world," though not exclusively so. The Church retains a constant relationship to God through its members by means of His immanence to the Church by His Spirit or grace.

[25] This is not to deny that certain normative and even constitutive elements of the Church, if not of salvation, flow from the Christ event itself, such as Scripture or the Eucharist. Moreover, the exact function of the whole Church in history will vary according to one's Christology. See Schineller, *art. cit.*, and Burns, *art. cit.*

a change in consciousness for those working at the frontier of the Church, on the boundary, as it were, between the Church and the non-Christian and secular "world," that has far outstripped the development of consciousness within the established churches.

If one allows the symbol of "mission" to command the context of reflection on the Church and makes it the point of departure for beginning to understand the Church as a whole, the result will be an ecclesiology considerably different from the traditional, even while remaining in close continuity with that tradition, especially scriptural tradition. This can be seen, for example, in the work of the late Johannes Hoekendijk.[26] For him, the nature of the Church, what the Church is, is completely determined by its role, its mission to and for the world, the participation in Christ's mission of proclaiming and helping to effect God's *shalom* in history. Hoekendijk moves a step further and embraces an "actualist" ecclesiology. The Church "*happens* insofar as it actually proclaims the Kingdom to the world."[27] A Church not engaged in such action is really only an empty shell, an empirical phenomenon to be sure, but not the authentic Church of Christ. This actualist position, I would take it, is valid as a theological ideal raised to the level of prophetic judgment. But the view is difficult to apply both empirically and ontologically. Every Church is institutional in some measure, and fidelity to Christ's mission is never perfect; one must take into account the fact that the Church is sinful. I will show below why an extreme actualist position need not be held.

From this functional point of view it would seem that Vatican II's Decree on the Church's Missionary Activity is a much more significant document than it is normally considered to be. First, though only a decree and not a dogmatic constitution, it argues dogmatically. It harks back to *Lumen gentium* and says that the Church is essentially and by its nature in a condition of mission. Moreover, it says that the whole Church, everywhere and in all its members, is missionary. Such is the intrinsic quality of the Christian life itself, and so of the life of the whole Church. Thus it defines a "nature" of the Church that is also essentially "functional" and outgoing to and for the world.

Church as Sign

The second major theological symbol that responds to the question "Why the Church?" is the concept of the Church as sacrament or sign. Canonized by Vatican II in several of its documents, some think it the most important theological achievement of the Council. One reason is

---

[26] See his *The Church Inside Out* (Philadelphia, 1966).
[27] *Ibid.*, p. 40.

the versatility of the symbol: it combines in a remarkable way theoretical understanding and concrete practical considerations; it unites the external and internal aspects of the Church, its communitarian and institutional dimensions; it unifies on a higher level within itself both word and sacrament; strategies of evangelization and development can be shown to be integrated within it, and so on. But most important for this discussion, the concept of sign, symbol, or sacrament combines "substance" and "function," community and mission, in an extraordinarily clear way.

When the theology of the Church as sign or sacrament was developed not many years ago (although the concept can be found in the patristic period), the concept did not have a very strong functional intentionality.[28] More and more, however, the functionality of the Church as sign is being explored to respond to the question of the Church's place in world history. Granted that the Church *is* a sign or sacrament, what is the *efficacy* of the sign? A sign is only a sign when it actually signifies. Given a concrete, existential, and historical point of view, and given the context of the world and the Church as mission to and for it, the question becomes, how should the Church go about its task of signifying? Granted the Church possesses grace—for in the Christian view the whole world is graced—the question remains of the specific role of the Church in signifying and demonstrating that truth. In this way the concept of the Church as sign is absorbed into the functionalist context of "mission" to the world, is rendered relational, and begins to operate existentially and dynamically, even while the "substantive" substructure is preserved. Thus the response to the substantive question of the Church remains intact: the Church *is* the community of faith, the Church *is* an institution, the Church *is* the Body of Christ and a sacrament. But the very purpose of this Church's existence in history is its mission. And once again the question of the Church is led back to one of credibility, how it should fulfil its mission.

Church Not in Service to Itself

As a conclusion to this part of the discussion, its logic leads inevitably to the affirmation that the Church is not primarily in service to itself. This statement represents the most radical shift for one's understanding of the Church today. It marks a certain about-face in relation to many ecclesiologies of the past. And yet it seems inescapable. A self-serving or self-preoccupied intentionality cannot explain an expansive primitive

[28] See Avery Dulles, *Models of the Church* (New York, 1974) pp. 58–70, for a brief overview of this understanding of the Church.

Church or a Paul. Rather, the Church from the beginning was in service of the *missio Dei*, and presumably the object of that is universal human history and the world. The Church is primarily in service to the world; it is sent to those outside itself. There is, of course, no need to interpret this exclusively; one need not deny that the Church is a community of worship and mutual support and nourishment in the faith.[29] But this aspect of the Church's life should always nourish and lead to the execution of the Church's primary mission.

Once again the point that is being made here must be clarified, since the issue is fundamental and has implications for two basic spiritualities which are at present polarizing the Roman Catholic Church.[30] On the level of everyday Christian living, there is no doubt that prayerful interiority and contact with God through Christ in communities are necessary to sustain an outgoing Christian service to the world. At this level there can be no question of priority, since the two movements are strictly reciprocal. Just as the human personality grows in responding to the other and can respond the better the more it grows in integral maturity, so it is with Christian life and the Church. What is being affirmed here, however, must be understood at a much deeper level. The question is one of understanding the very purpose of the Church, its *raison d'être* in history. God's revelation is mediated in and through people in this world. The purpose of the Church's existence is the world to which it is sent, because it is the continuing agent of God's revelation rendering it actual and available to other people. The ground for this position is Christological, then, but not simply in the sense that the Church is to be patterned after the historical Jesus as the "man for others,"[31] which indeed it should. Rather, the Church finds its ground of being in the event of Christ as a "mission" and revelation from God to the world in history. A continuing response to God through Jesus Christ is therefore essential and constitutive of the Church, but in this conception it is not an end in itself; for what is at stake is precisely the quality of that response to God through Christ. To be Christian and to be Church means to be "chosen" for service to continue the work of Christ in the world. This outward orientation to the world thus becomes a

[29] For the Church as community united by Trinitarian love, see Sears, *art. cit.* This substantive view of the Church is accepted here as a presupposition; the Church *is* a community *for* mission.

[30] The reference is, on the one hand, to the charismatic and prayer movements, and on the other, to the growing concern for social engagement on the part of the Church.

[31] The assertion that the only significance of Jesus is that he should be imitated, and the sole reason for the Church is to generate followers who lived as he did, would result in a Christology and ecclesiology of Schineller's fourth type.

determinative factor in Christian spirituality, a criterion, and this in a final (teleological) way.[32]

THE CHURCH IN TODAY'S WORLD

We have seen the humanist critique of what it takes to be the necessary failure of the Church to become immanent to the world, and the Church's failure at transcendence in its being-in-the-world. We have also seen how a reconstruction of an understanding of the Church might begin by taking that critique seriously, while at the same time using traditional symbols and contemporary theological insights. In this section I want to sketch how some of the theological data already presented might be brought to bear on the problem of the Church in such a way as to generate a coherent understanding of the nature and function of the Church that also responds to that problem.

Knowledge and Action

Ultimately, the problem of the Church as organization and institution is one of credibility, and this is a moral and political problem.[33] Both the problem of the Church and the problem of understanding the Church are grounded in the behavior of the Church in the world. The final response to the question of the Church can be none other than performance, and this is the case not only for those standing outside the Church and observing it, but also for the Christian. To begin, then, a brief reflection on the relation between knowledge and action is necessary.

Knowledge and behavior are intimately related. Because the human person is one, there is a point where understanding or knowing and action converge in personal existence. In the total life of the person, knowledge on all its levels is for action, and action in its turn informs knowledge. Just as knowing is itself a form of action, so human action in all its forms

---

[32] This is confirmed both by Matthew's Gospel and in Luke–Acts. See William Thompson and Eugene LaVerdiere, "New Testament Communities in Transition: A Study of Matthew and Luke," earlier in this issue. Relative to the Christologies developed in Schineller's article, this ecclesiology may be seen to flow from either his second, a constitutive and normative Christology, or his third, a normative but nonconstitutive Christology. In a constitutive Christology, however, because the exalted unique and divine status of Christ is so prominent, there is danger that Christian attention be so focused on his person that his will or mandate for his followers be slighted. The danger is that the Christian experiences his relationship to Christ in and for itself and not as including the element of being chosen for mission.

[33] Even though the word "political" is ambiguous, I continue to use it because none other is as exact. "Politics" here does not have the narrow meaning of running civil government; much less does it mean dealing "behind the scenes" or in "back rooms." It refers simply to people both in official capacities and unofficial positions managing their public affairs in whatever sphere.

is a kind of knowing: its inner logic and response contain an implicit or more or less explicit unveiling of the object of response, of reality.

This brief analysis, however, can be pushed considerably further to show how knowledge really depends on the will, that is, on decision and action. This insight was developed by Blondel in *L'Action*[34] and is especially relevant in religious matters. A distinction must be made between "notional" knowledge, a coherent set of concepts or symbols, no matter how objective in themselves, and "possessive" knowledge. The problematic in the distinction between these two kinds of knowledge does not lie in the relation between ideas and their correspondence to reality, or between subjective experience and objective knowledge. The question is whether or not a person enters into a qualitatively different relationship, an actual and existential relationship, with the reality that ideas happen to express. Ultimately, only action can mediate this passage; possessive knowledge is a function of a willing or choosing what is known and putting that "knowledge" into act. "That which was simply an idea of the object becomes, in complete truth, an objective certitude and a real possession."[35] Action, especially in relation to that which is finally transcendent, is that which alone can mediate a real or existential or possessive knowledge. Action in that sense, then, is the final criterion of religious knowledge. In the realm of personal affirmation of truth, it is the ultimate and necessary criterion; in the public realm, that is, in the mediation of truth to others, it is a necessary but not necessitating criterion.

In the light of this principle, that action is the final criterion of validity and truth, what performance is necessary to "demonstrate" the truth of the Church, its immanence and transcendence, to those outside? How is the Church to be a valid sign to the world to which it is sent? More importantly, what action is demanded by the Church to validate its claims *to its own members*, that is, to itself? Working from the principle that action and understanding are mutually determinative, the theological question of the Church in today's world becomes a reciprocally related double question: What understanding of the Church is necessary to mediate her performance in the world, and what understanding is necessitated by the action that is demanded of the Church by the world?

[34] Maurice Blondel, *L'Action: Essai d'une critique de la vie et d'une science de la pratique* (Paris, 1893 and 1950). I have sketched the development of Blondel's early thought in "The Unfolding of Modernism in France: Blondel, Laberthonnière, Le Roy," THEOLOGICAL STUDIES 35 (1974) 632–66.

[35] *Op. cit.*, p. 440. This distinction is not to be confused with Newman's notional vs. real assent. The point here is quite different. In Newman, the point of the distinction is the quality of the apprehension and assent. In Blondel, the point is the existential engagement with and possession of the reality in both apprehension and assent, or the lack of this.

Church and World

The term "world" has always been ambiguous in Christian vocabulary. The term is used here in two senses. In the first place, the symbol
"world" refers to the field of human activity; it is the empirical universe,
especially our planet; it is our world, with the people in it and with a
special reference to human history and culture. In a second and rather
uniquely Christian sense, "the world" refers to non-Christians. Those
who are not inside the Church, both those who embrace other religions
than Christianity and those who live in an "unchurched" sphere of
existence, are often implicitly designated by the Christian use of "world."
In neither case, however, does the symbol "world" have the pejorative
sense it sometimes receives in John's Gospel. But neither is that
pejorative sense excluded. There is sin in the world, and an uncritical
view of the world is alien to Christianity and secular culture alike.[36] But
the world and sin are not and should not be considered synonymous. If
there is sin in the world, there is also sin in the Church,[37] so that the
element of sin cannot be held as a point of differentiation between the
Church and the world.

In the Christian view of things the world is not negative, nor is it
neutral; ultimately, the world in both senses must be viewed positively.
The doctrines of creation, providence, and redemption portray the one
world and the one history of the race, the only world and the only history
we have, as salvific. "Where sin increased, grace abounded all the
more."[38] Here again a concrete historical and existential theology must
view the action of God's providence and grace in the world in a way that
disallows all sharply dualistic conceptions of nature and grace, the
kingdom of God and the kingdom of man, the religious and the secular;
for if one admits a universal salvific will of God, which traditional
Christianity by and large has, then one must also view the whole human
sphere (the world in both senses) as positively under the influence of
God's grace. In no way, then, except as a rejection of grace which is sin,
can the world or life in it be viewed negatively. The world and human

[36] See David Tracy, *Blessed Rage for Order* (New York, 1975) pp. 10–14.

[37] See Karl Rahner, "The Church of Sinners" and "The Sinful Church in the Decrees of
Vatican II," *Theological Investigations* 6 (Baltimore, 1969) 253–69, 270–94.

[38] Rom 5:20. The following position of Karl Rahner may be considered a commentary on
this text: "It is furthermore impossible that this offer of supernatural, divinizing grace
made to all men on account of the universal salvific purpose of God, should in general
(prescinding from the relatively few exceptions) remain ineffective in most cases on account
of the personal guilt of the individual. For, as far as the gospel is concerned, we have no
really conclusive reason for thinking so pessimistically of men. On the other hand, and
contrary to every merely human experience, we do have every reason for thinking
optimistically of God and his salvific will which is more powerful than the extremely
limited stupidity and evil-mindedness of men" ("Christianity and the Non-Christian
Religions," *Theological Investigations* 5 [Baltimore, 1966] 123).

history are grounded in an offer of salvation, and it is here and only here that salvation is accomplished.

Once this totally negative view of the world as intrinsically evil in itself is cleared away, one is free to look upon the relation of the Church to the world in more positive terms. In the first place, when the world is conceived as the empirical sphere of human activity, the Church must be seen as integrally part of this world. As long as it exists, the Church simply *is* a more or less influential part of human history sheerly on the practical level of matter of fact. But over and above this, the sociology of religion has shown that religion, and therefore the Church, tends to be the preserver and guarantor of the more profound meanings and values of culture, a role which Tillich, on a deeper level, has termed "the substance of culture."[39] In short, whether the Church is active or passive in relation to the world, it plays a vital and inescapable role in the world and its history.

The Church is also intrinsically and positively related to the world when "world" is understood as the sphere of non-Christians or those outside the Church. This is so because ultimately the Church is the institutionalization of Christian faith and the Christian life. This Christian faith, however, involves as essential elements the love of God and the love of neighbor in such a way that the two are inextricably united and cannot be considered separable.[40] It follows, then, that the Church, as the whole body or community of those who share the same faith, must assume in its institutionalized and communitarian forms the same characteristics of love of neighbor relative to the world; for it is in this way that the institutional aspect of the Church fosters and supports the inner dynamism of its own life of faith and at the same time renders it visible and public.[41]

[39] Paul Tillich, *Theology of Culture* (New York, 1964) pp. 40–43.

[40] Karl Rahner, "Reflections on the Unity of the Love of Neighbour and the Love of God," *Theological Investigations* 6 (Baltimore, 1969) 231–49.

[41] This argument will be developed further in a later portion of my essay. The importance of the principle should not be lost because of the brevity of the statement here. Much of the theology of liberation, as well as related themes of "development" in mission theology, ultimately rest on the essential place of love of neighbor in Christian life. These theologies, insofar as they are "theologies," do not rest on a Marxist view of reality or a sociology of revolution. I agree with John A. Coleman that there must be "a theory of the middle range," an economic, political, and social ethics, to mediate between a Christian view of history and concrete political action. "Liberation theology must become much more a social ethics than it has so far, if it is going to be an effective instrument in suggesting concrete political praxis" ("Vision and Praxis in American Theology: Orestes Brownson, John A. Ryan, and John Courtney Murray," THEOLOGICAL STUDIES 37 [1976] 32–33). But here we are dealing with the prior question of why the Church should be concerned with the world at all, and how it should conceive its relationship to it. See, finally, the fourth and highest level of Church existence in Sears's article "Trinitarian Love as Ground of the Church."

In sum, both the world and the Church's relation to it must be viewed positively. Moreover, the Church is as a matter of fact and should be actively engaged in this world. But exactly how is this involvement to be understood, and how is the Church to be understood in such a way that this active and positive relation is protected and nourished?

Church as Mission to World

The symbol "mission" releases a whole set of closely interrelated meanings which are all cognate to the basic idea of "being sent." The symbol thus discloses a Church that exists as an intrinsically and essentially dynamic, expansive, and outward-oriented community.[42] The Church as mission would be a community of people with a "commission," those who have received a mandate and hence exist with an inner obligation or responsibility to fulfil that which they are sent *for* related to those they are sent *to*. Without developing this symbol fully—for this is not the purpose here—it may be said, first, that the object of the mission of the Church is the world in the sense that it is to the world that it is sent. Secondly, the object of the mission in the sense of its purpose is to be a sign to and for the world of what it has received from Christ. The first object of the mission will be developed in this section, the second in the following section.

The Church *is* mission, and it is mission to the world. In this statement the radicality of the symbol begins to appear. Adrian Hastings has put it succinctly:

It is, therefore, somewhat misleading to say that the Church has a mission, as if the existence of the Church comes first. In truth it is because of the mission that there is a Church; the Church is the servant and expression of the mission. The mission consequently dictates the nature of the Church and in so far as the Church fails to live up to the demands of mission, it is effectively failing to be Church.[43]

[42] The symbol "mission" is not to be confused or identified with the term "missionary." The missionary movement is only one form of the outward-oriented and expansive nature of the Church. Missionary expansion has dominated the understanding of the Church's mission in the past, and it is still significant, but it will become increasingly less so as the so-called "one world" phenomenon increases—which is to say, as more and more areas and cultures are exposed to a Christian presence, witness, and influence. But the symbol will always retain its significance as dictating an outward turning toward the world.

[43] Adrian Hastings, "Mission," *Encyclopedia of Theology: The Concise Sacramentum Mundi*, ed. Karl Rahner (New York, 1975) p. 968. See Thompson's essay, where the emergent self-understanding of the Matthean Church was based on the idea of "mission," and LaVerdiere, where the universality of the Church and the mission towards Rome is a constant throughout Luke–Acts. In both, the very purpose of the Church is to continue the mission of Jesus to the whole world.

The object of this mission, those to whom this Church is sent, is the world; the Church is sent to people in history. The Church's existence is thus defined as intrinsically oriented towards the world in the sense of those people outside itself. In being thus defined, the Church is firmly rooted in a religious conception that is fundamental to the Old Testament and the New and is continued in the tradition of Augustine and Aquinas: God works in history through human agents, revelation is mediated to history through what is classically called "economy." From this it follows that, although the empirical or phenomenal object of the Church's mission is the world in all its temporality and secularity, there can be no confusion of the Church with other agents of social ameliora-tion. The Church is not the World Bank or Rotary International. Rather, it is both drawn and driven forward by the *missio Dei* as this has been revealed in Jesus the Christ.

This symbol is proposed here as fundamental and all-embracing for understanding the Church today. This does not mean that there is not or should not be pluralism in understanding the Church. In *Models of the Church* Avery Dulles has demonstrated by typology that several different understandings of the Church coexist among Christians at the same time. The symbol "mission" does not negate this pluralism but tran-scends it. As an expression of the fundamental reason for the Church's existence the symbol of "mission" is an a priori which includes more specific models within itself and at the same time is a criterion for judging them. Pluralism is a healthy phenomenon so long as it is set in a wider context of a unified and basic intention; only then will pluralism be neither divisive not debilitating. Theoretically, then, "mission" is *the* biblical symbol adequate for understanding the Church in relation to the world today, given the problem it faces.[44] And practically speaking, in terms of action, without such a common understanding the Church will stand helpless, divided, and inactive in the face of social situations which require its response.

The proposition that the symbol "mission" is the all-embracive category for understanding the Church today involves a constant tension between two principles. On the one hand, what James Gustafson has called "thematic unitarianism," or what might also be termed "thematic monophysitism," must be avoided: "By a thematic unitarianism I mean the isolation, accentuation, and even the exclusive concentration upon a

---

[44] The symbol "mission" is thus proposed as meeting the double "criterion of adequacy" to common contemporary experience and "criterion of appropriateness" to the scriptural understanding of the Church. See Tracy, *op. cit.*, pp. 64–87. See also his "The Task of Fundamental Theology," *Journal of Religion* 54 (1975) 13–33.

single theological theme (such as liberation), a single moral imperative
(such as the imperative to love), or a single technique for 'salvation'
(such as the human potential movement)."[45] The theology of the
Church, he continues, is multitextured and multivalent, just as human
life is multidimensional. On the other hand, one must seek for unity and
coherence in one's understanding of the Church, and this involves
choosing centers of focus and organizing the dimensions of the Church in
relation to one another. For the Church to act in the world and not simply
exist, it must discern priorities among values and respond to imperatives. In the light of this tension, therefore, the symbol "mission" is not
proposed as exclusive but as inclusive, comprehensive, and all-encom-
passing. Although it is traditional, its dynamic quality responds to the
urgent experience and problem of the contemporary world, namely,
human responsibility in handling not simply nature but, more importantly, human relationships in history. Although this problem has not
been described at any length—for this would require a detailed analysis
of contemporary historical consciousness and the rising expectations of
the masses of the disenfranchised of this earth—the thesis proposed
depends on the recognition of this as the crisis of our times, the crisis of
the meaning of history, and on the conviction that Christianity has
spiritual resources to contribute to meeting it on a variety of levels. The
problem of the world thus becomes the problem of the Church and its
self-understanding. The tension within the life of the Church today lies
in a new call to draw upon the multidimensional resources of its inner
and transcendent spiritual life and to turn with these toward the world.
"Mission" is a category for understanding which may allow this to
happen.

Finally, Vatican II has laid the groundwork for such a self-understanding of the Church in Roman Catholicism, as can be illustrated in its
statement on the Church as mission. In this document the symbol
"mission" is viewed as totally encompassing the Church, and this can be
seen in four distinct but interrelated assertions. First, each Christian,
every single person in the Church, shares a mission responsibility.[46]
Second, the Church as a whole corporation or community or institution is
a mission.[47] Third, the Church is essentially a mission; this is what the
Church is by its very nature. Mission constitutes the "basic duty of the
People of God." [48] Therefore, fourth, wherever the Church is, mission is at

[45] James M. Gustafson, "What Ought to Be the Issue for Religion in American Society in
the 1980's," *Chicago Seminary Register* 65 (1975) 4.

[46] Constitution on the Church, no. 17 (*The Documents of Vatican II*, ed. W. M. Abbott
[New York, 1966] p. 36); Decree on the Church's Missionary Activity, nos. 23, 36
(*Documents*, pp. 613, 623).

[47] Decree on the Church's Missionary Activity, no. 35 (*Documents*, p. 623).

[48] *Ibid.*, nos. 35, 2 (*Documents*, pp. 623, 585).

the very center of its inner life; it is not to be conceived as something going on at the borders or periphery of the Church. The Church is never "established" so that mission ceases. Every local church or parish congregation is mission, so that it keeps on going out to the world, to fellow citizens and human beings, to the men and women who live around them.[49] The mission that is the Church does not cease.[50]

Church as Sign

The Church's nature and role is clarified further by looking at the meaning of the symbol "mission to the world" in terms of the purpose of the mission. Here the image or concept of sacrament or sign may be usefully employed. For the Christian, Jesus Christ is the normative revelation in history of God and the purpose of the world and the meaning of its history. Christ is the final revelation of sin and of grace. This means that the present condition of this world is not what it should be (sin), nor does it have to be what it is at present; rather, by God's power (grace) the world and history can be re-created and, in the end, will be. The purpose of the Church, its mission, is to continue to "body forth" in a visible and audible way in the world that very revelation it has accepted through faith and in Jesus.

As was said earlier, this faith that underlies the Christian life becomes sign to the world in a public and corporate way precisely in its institutionalization. The notion of the Church as sign or sacrament is neither abstract nor ethereal. The Church is sign, symbol, or sacrament precisely in its visible, organized, and institutional forms in history. The Church is a sign in its institutions, in its public functions and interventions in history, in the commitment of its resources and personnel, the way its members live their lives, by the focus of its energies through its leaders, in its buildings and budgets. Moreover, in terms of the truth and credibility of the Church as mission, of its immanence and transcendence, the notion of sign and sacrament is concrete, practical, and existential; and it has a critical relevance in the sense that people both outside and inside the Church understand it when they see it and are scandalized when they do not.[51]

[49] Ibid., no. 15 (Documents, pp. 602–3).
[50] Ibid., no. 6 (Documents, pp. 590–92).
[51] The practical relevance of this conception of the Church as sacrament or sign can be illustrated by an example. If a large city diocese in the United States were to close forty parish schools within the city in the course of a decade, and substantially cut back its financial support to the parishes in the inner city which are poor and whose territory included a population that was largely not Catholic, and were it to express publicly that its policy was to move its support to the suburbs where its main constituency had migrated, given the general problems of the cities in this country and by the criteria envisaged here, namely, mission and active sign-bearing, such a Church would simply not be credible. As an institution, it would be an actual countersign of the Christian life. One might say that

When the Church is understood as a sign in the dynamic and functional context of its mission to the world, and when it is viewed from a concrete, existential, and historical point of view, this understanding takes on a powerful and critical significance. Negatively, it leads to the conclusion that a sign is not a sign unless it actively signifies. A Church whose nature is sign-bearing but which does not actually or actively signify what it professes becomes by definition a countersign. It evacuates Christian words of their meaning and empties them of their value. And it must be admitted that historically and concretely any Christian Church at any particular time, any Christian communion, or particular church, or local church, or religious community can become a countersign to its particular milieu and in effect lead people away from Christ. Furthermore, once the dynamism of the sign is taken seriously and viewed empirically, it follows that the institutional aspects of the Church can no longer be viewed in themselves but must be judged in the light of their efficacy for the sign-mission. Positively, this understanding, when viewed concretely and historically, means that the credibility and the truth of the Church really depend on its actual ability to exercise its transcendence within the world. The freedom, communion, transcendence, and holiness which are the marks of the Christian life will only become *real* in the Church when they are embodied concretely in it as a community of people and as an institution, so that the mission of Christ might be actually continued in a public and historical way.

Once again, the Vatican Council addressed this issue of the purpose of mission in terms of how the Church was to fulfil its mission to the world for Roman Catholicism. The world to and for which the Church is mission was viewed historically and concretely by the Council. Thus the mission of the Church is to be carried out in different ways according to the concrete situation and circumstance of the people addressed, and these will be many and varied.[52] In many places it may not be profitable to simply expound the gospel directly and immediately. In such circumstances the Church should "bear witness to Christ by charity and works of mercy, with all patience, prudence, and great confidence."[53] In

---

the Church as an ontological sign survived in the institution because of its historical continuity with the past and through other less visible apostolic actions. And the authentic Church would certainly be alive in the community that subsisted partly within, partly beside, and partly prescinding from the institution's leadership. But as an institution called "Church," such a Church would be a scandal to many within her. And those outside this Church who were dedicated to the amelioration of the life of the poor would undoubtedly count this Church as an enemy, or at least no ally—and rightly so if this movement continued.

[52] Decree on the Church's Missionary Activity, no. 6 (*Documents*, pp. 590–92).

[53] *Ibid.*

this way the Council recognized that the fundamental and deepest exigency is that the Church, through the work of its members and in its official representatives and structures, become thoroughly involved in the everyday life and problems of the people, immersed in their culture, and dedicated to their needs, and all this primarily by action. Such a course obviously does not preclude preaching and accepting converts. When this happens, Christians who have a natural desire to share and communicate what they have themselves received as a gift will certainly rejoice. But the first and primary task of the Church is that of just being there as a concrete sign of the love of God for all people. This commitment to developmental work, to the work of humanization, to the simple love of one's fellow men and women is thus conceived as an essential and integral part of what has classically been understood as the evangelization process—as indeed one might expect, since in teaching this the Council added nothing to the teaching of Jesus in the parable of the Good Samaritan.[54] Moreover, it took this to be the concrete test of the credibility of the Church's message.[55]

Holiness and Mission Spirituality

We must consider, finally, the faith life of the sign-bearing mission Church. Christian tradition has always maintained that there is an intimate connection between faith in God and love of neighbor. It can be argued both systematically and from Scripture that the two, if authentically possessed, merge into identity at the deepest level of the personality. The neighbor, of course, is the other, the fellow human being who, though not part of "my own" and perhaps not even "worthy" of my love, demands it of me in faith because of his own intrinsic and infinite value grounded in the common creative and accepting love of the Father. Christian faith, then, and the Christian life have a necessary and internal orientation of service outside the self and into the world of other people. In a sense, this is the empirical and this-worldly test of faith's transcendence. And it is axiomatic that a love which is not expressed in some form of action is no love at all. In the light of the problem of the Church, these absolutely fundamental principles concerning faith take on new and enormously important relevance.

Holiness or sanctity can be nothing else than this Christian life of faith led to an exceptional degree of integrity. This is something to which

---

[54] This was made explicit by the 1971 Synod of Bishops in the following famous sentence: "Action on behalf of justice and participation in the transformation of the world fully appear to us as a constitutive dimension of the preaching of the Gospel, or, in other words, of the Church's mission for the redemption of the human race and its liberation from every oppressive situation."

[55] See Decree on the Church's Missionary Activity, nos. 11–12 (*Documents*, pp. 597–99).

all Christians are called, and there can be no class distinctions at this level, no double standards of sanctity. Viewed from a concrete, existential, and historical point of view, there can be no ontological "states" or "offices" of perfection or holiness; holiness can only exist as a moral quality of a person.[56]

The Church is the community of the faithful called to lead a Christian life of holiness; it is the "people of God." The Church is not in its first moment an institution. One cannot imagine a Church institution independently of a prior people of faith. Genetically and structurally, the Church is the coming together of people who in faith are grasped by God as manifested in Jesus the Christ. Institutions gradually emerged to give form to the community's life in the Spirit, as would happen in any other community. Thus this people of God *is* institutionalized, and sociologically it had to be. The Church as institution is the institutionalization of the Spirit-inspired faith life of the people of God. If the Church is the institutionalization of the Christian life, then the Church as corporation, identifiable community, and institution must take on the character of the action-oriented Christian love of neighbor that is internal to and constitutive of authentic faith. The understanding of the Church must be such that as an institution it is not only coherent with but also structures and nourishes the selfless Christian life of which it is the institutionalization. Reciprocally, views of holiness or Christian perfection must be influenced, indeed determined, by the understanding or theology of the Church. In other words, Christian spirituality should be ecclesial,[57] and consequently it should be mission spirituality.

The importance of this question of holiness and spirituality cannot be exaggerated in any discussion of the Church. Conceptions of holiness are as culturally determined as any other conceptions, but it often seems

[56] Regarding the Church, Hans Küng writes: "The New Testament knows nothing of institutional sanctity, of a sacred 'it'; it does not speak of a Church which invests as many of its institutions, places, times and implements as possible with the attribute 'holy.' The only kind of holiness at issue here is a completely *personal* sanctity" (*The Church* [New York, 1967] p. 325). One may agree with Küng here because of that against which he is reacting. At the same time, both his statement and our statement in the text must be qualified; for all human activity can be imitated, patterned, objectified, and institutionalized. On this basis one may speak paradoxically both of institutional grace and of institutional sin. What must be constantly recalled, however, is that all such objectifications and institutionalizations have their basic ground and stuff in human, and hence subjective and moral, activity. At the same time, precisely insofar as this human activity is routinized and objectified, it may lose both its consciously religious quality and its consciously sinful quality.

[57] Thus Gregory Baum writes: "The fellowship the Open Church creates among her members and the holiness into which she initiates them are subordinated to the transforming effect of the Christian community on the society in which it lives" (*The Credibility of the Church Today*, p. 197).

that the Church's conceptions of holiness and sanctity are still determined by dated models from the past and are not being informed by
theological exigencies that are radically new.[58] Christian spirituality or
piety must involve one's active participation in the world of the
everyday. As a matter of fact, the vast majority of the time of the vast
majority of Christians is spent immersed in the world, and this activity is
not unrelated to either personal sanctity, salvation, or Christian mission.
This implies the exigency today for a concept of holiness that places the
Christian in the world and makes him as a Christian just as responsible
for what goes on there as anyone else. Given the commandment of love of
neighbor, and given our heightened awareness of people in need and the
new technical ability to do something about it, Christian spirituality
should examine critically and theologically those forms of Christian life
and ideals of holiness that seem to involve drawing a person or
community out of this world and cutting off all relations with other
people. Prayer, sacramental practice, and worship itself if they are closed
off from love of neighbor, mysticism if it is escapist, monasticism and
other forms of religious community if they are turned inward upon
themselves, suddenly appear in today's culture as ambiguous and
inauthentically Christian. It cannot be presumed that union with God
which involves a neglect of responsibility in this world and for this world
has anything to do with Christian holiness.[59] And as far as any renewed
understanding of the Church is concerned, unless the language, symbols,
and understanding of the ideal Christian life change, current ecclesiology
will have little impact on anyone.[60]

CONCLUSION

The question of the Church today is a real one, and the problem of
understanding the Church is a real problem. It has been suggested here
that the problem is at the same time practical, moral, and profoundly
theological; it is a problem of credibility stemming from a failure in
action which is in its turn rooted in theological understanding. Relative
to life in this world and responsibility for addressing the grave social

[58] One thinks of the lives of many (not all) of the saints who are presently venerated,
whose total lives (as opposed to one or other aspect of them) not only fail to provide models
within our culture but may also be symbolically counterproductive of the kind of
spirituality demanded today.

[59] We have opened up a very complex question here. Many presuppositions are involved,
such as the nature of history and eschatology (Is history continuous or discontinuous with
the "end-time"?), the Christian conception of God (Is God jealous of man's constant
attention or has He released the race into history in freedom as a task for responsible
creativity?), the Pelagian question, and so on. Unfortunately, these questions cannot be
dealt with here.

[60] See Michael C. Reilly, "Holiness and Development," *America* 133 (1975) 204-7.

issues of our time, the data would seem to indicate that being a Church member does not make any difference, or worse, the sphere of the Church protects one from having to assume responsibility for these issues. If that is the case in any particular Church, it may be better for any given person that he or she lead his or her Christian life outside and apart from that Church, and in another; for this remains a definite possibility in our pluralistic situation. It also happens that a person's ultimate convictions about reality and God can today remain profoundly Christian while one seeks a more personal identity through other forms of community and voluntary association. Or one could remain within the Church and remain as well profoundly indifferent to its institutional life. This too is a common stance, and it is becoming more common.[61] What these phenomena point to is the fact that the problem of the Church today is one of credibility not only for non-Christians but also for Christians, and it can be described in distinctly political terms.[62]

But the sphere of politics and action is not purely pragmatic. Action and behavior and responsibility and decision imply understanding. The question of the Church, therefore, is posed to theological understanding, reasoning, and judgment, and it must be posed on the most basic level of the very nature and role of the Christian life and its institutionalization in history which is the Church. But this question of the Church must be posed today in such a way that, from the very beginning, it is addressed in relation to this world, to life in it and responsibility for it. Unless that is done, the Church will be entrapped within a self-enclosed self-understanding and will ultimately be understood on the basis of a personal assurance of salvation or, even worse, in such shallow terms as "It is my home" and "I feel secure there."

Finally, I have argued that the Church has had and does possess the symbol of self-understanding that both absorbs into itself the contemporary critique of the Church and responds to it confidently in a uniquely

---

[61] An individualistic faith-life is, of course, both "unnatural," because of the social nature of the human person, and contrary to the inner dynamism of Christian faith itself. A person who leaves the Church may be deserting precisely the mission of the Church. It is for these reasons that the phenomenon may be seen as a critique and should be so disturbing for the churches.

[62] This statement does not entail a reduction of the religious to the moral sphere. The two are distinct but cannot be separated. Only to the degree that one sees how closely these two spheres are related will it be appreciated why the root of the crisis of the Church is moral and why this also involves a theological problem of understanding. I have used the practical problems of behavior and credibility as the point of entry into the theological problem of the Church precisely because, on the one hand, decision and action cannot be separated from understanding, and on the other, inversely, theology does make a difference for Church policy and decision. One must pass from sociological and political data to the deeper theological issues.

traditional and Christic way. That symbol is "mission."[63] As was the mission of Christ, so the Church is sent to the world and for the world, especially the dispossessed, to help make all things new in the name of Christ.

COMMENTS ON ROGER D. HAIGHT'S ARTICLE

In a joint issue on Church a question will inevitably emerge: How would the two systematic positions on "Why the Church?" respond to each other? This comment attempts an answer to the legitimate request, and thus presupposes some acquaintance with my article "Trinitarian Love as Ground of the Church."

Haight's choice of "mission" as symbol for understanding the Church not only responds to an empirical tendency of our day to "Show me," but also calls the Church to a much-needed conversion from complacency and institutional in-turning to examine itself for signs of real self-transcendence in the form of service to the world. He takes the world seriously, both as a place where God's grace acts and as being in need of the Church's service of love. On all of these points there is basic agreement between us.

The difference between our two positions appears both in our points of departure and in our underlying philosophies. Haight begins with the problematic the modern world gives us—pragmatic, empirical, aware of historical relativity. Scripture is appealed to as responding to that problematic. In my view, our present culture not only provides new possibilities of understanding Scripture; it is also called into question by Scripture. In some ways we always fall short of God's revelation in Christ, and we have to look to that source to judge even our own time. As I see it, present-day inadequacy is manifested in our very tendency to think only functionally and empirically, with the result that permanent commitments—whether in marriage or the churches—are being progressively

---

[63] Michael A. Fahey, S.J., in "The Mission of the Church: To Divinize or Humanize?" (address to the national convention of the Catholic Theological Society of America, June 1976; will appear soon in the *Proceedings*), assumes a concrete and realistic perspective, examines the shifts in the meaning of the term "mission" through history, and reacts against the sudden escalation in its usage over the past couple of decades together with its inflation to include too many different roles for the Church in the world. His point is that specific tasks or any single activity among many should not be identified with *the* mission of the Church. It would be better to speak of the "tasks" of the Church. He then constructively explores the new meaning contained in the idea of the *munus* of the Church, a term employed in Vatican II's *Gaudium et spes*. He concludes that the Church has several areas of responsibility outside itself to the non-Christ-confessing world even after the gospel has been announced. These areas correspond to the "integrational, prophetic, and eschatological" functions or dimensions of the Church. I would agree that "mission" can be and has been abused and cheapened, especially when it is used in everyday descriptive and inspirational language about the activities or agenda of the Church. However, as a theological symbol that opens up meaning and mediates understanding, it can help to link the qualities of Vatican II's *munus* with the New Testament and tradition, can help to ground those qualities therein. On this level, and for this reason, I think Fahey would agree that the symbol should not be abandoned but rather explored even further.

undermined because of our inability to face the inevitable dark and unrewarding times such commitments entail. If Christ has won a final victory, the Church's participation in that victory must somehow be valid for all time. How it will be lived out in any age certainly changes, but the basic structure of committed communal love remains constant. In my view, the most pressing need of the Church today is to rediscover that spiritual groundwork as the basis for any solid missionary work.

As for our philosophies, Haight appeals to empiricism and functionalism as most suitable for today's mentality. My position looks to empirical data, especially that of depth psychology, but is unabashedly ontological—and, indeed, with an interpersonal ontology. Empiricism thinks from the outside in, looks for marks of credibility and functional effect. An interpersonal ontology thinks from the inside out, to discover the energy sources from which the outer effect will be lasting and fruitful. Both are needed. Without looking to outward effect, inner dynamics will stagnate in mere process; but unless the interpersonal dynamic is attended to, our social action will collapse through lack of staying power. Contrary to Haight, my view of our present problem is that inner dynamics are most neglected, and that unless we rediscover spiritual growth and community, a mission-oriented approach is in danger of perpetuating our present alienation from self-understanding, much as the Protestant churches are discovering the inadequacy of a merely social gospel in our day.

It is the difference in philosophies that determines our different views of finality in the Church. Haight sees one overarching finality, that of mission. I have affirmed a double finality, like that of marriage. As conjugal love and procreation of children are both seen as ends of marriage, so I see Christian community and mission as double ends of the Church. Haight's view corresponds to a functional philosophy; it has the efficiency of one goal that can clearly direct decisions. My view follows from an interpersonal ontology in which persons are never means to an end. Since our union with Christ and community is already an end—much like the love of spouses—it cannot be subordinated to mission, even though its authenticity is revealed in the desire to communicate this love to others. A Trinitarian view is at home with such a complex finality, since it reflects the different processions in the Trinity. These different positions are not without implications for decisions. For me, the Church does have a mission to itself, its own conversion and growth. Hence a spirituality serving deeper relation to God—even monastic spirituality—may ever be needed to empower the other finality of mission. Further, a double finality is not solely focused on the transcendent kingdom; it celebrates the present kingdom, and out of this celebration is motivated to give with joy what it has found. This view sees in the community a love that "never ends," so that all attention is not simply focused on the "not yet" of mission.

Thus I see "mission" as but one aspect of the complex goal of the Church. If the total goal is not kept in mind, it seems to me we will be consigned to a recurrent dialectic from one neglected aspect to another, without being rooted in an adequate overview. "Mission" itself will differ according to particular needs. The present need is most likely what Haight sees—to extend the service of God's love to the oppressed and neglected. But liberation itself is only a beginning. One needs to build committed community and to transform the world in final submission to God. The world may reject this, since a God-centered, communal view demands the cross, but the Church cannot tailor its call to what the world is ready to accept. The Church's call may be as mysterious as that of a Mother Teresa of Calcutta, which calls the world out of its own self-centered ends to a recognition that beyond all, and relativizing all, is the eternal community with God and fellow believers that all our hopes are grounded in and foreshadow.

ROBERT T. SEARS, S.J.

V

TRINITARIAN LOVE AS GROUND OF THE CHURCH

ROBERT T. SEARS, S.J.

Jesuit School of Theology in Chicago

THE CONCEPT of "anonymous Christianity" and the possibility of grace outside the limits of the visible Church has forced Catholics to reappraise the question "Why the Church?" When we allow with Vatican II the movement of God's kingdom within the world as a whole, the focus of the theological understanding of history moves from the Church, the Mystical Body in the making, to the world, and the dictum "Outside the Church no salvation" simply appears anachronistic.[1] At the same time, our experience-centered age is listening to the humanists' question whether the Church is not removing its members from active involvement in the development of the world, and to the liberationists' query whether personal freedom is not oppressed by authoritarian structures. Church membership declines as many see the possibility of living Christian lives outside the Church or prescinding from its directives.

One response to the new question "Why the Church?" is to focus on a functional understanding of Church in terms of its mission to the world to be an explicit "sign" of God's love which in principle is operative in the world as a whole.[2] Such a position would not require a large church, for it would remain meaningful despite the phenomenon of decreasing Church membership in our modern secularized age. To be credible to the world, such a "sign" demands personal and communal conversion to a mission-oriented spirituality. The Church as institution is meaningful to the extent that it structures this service of love and thus continues Christ's mission of making God's love credible in the world.

As important as this focus on mission is, it raises a theological difficulty: Who is to judge whether or not God's love is really being revealed? To be a "sign," one must know what is to be signified. If one emphasizes credibility to the world as a principle for the Church's own self-understanding, this would seem to make the world—which is at least not explicitly aware of the Christian nature of this love—the judge of whether or not the Church is really living God's love. But God's love is not simply a response to human needs, though it is this at the deepest level of need for God. It is a call to faith in His kingdom, and as Paul remarks to the Corinthians, "no one knows what lies at the depths of God but the Spirit of God" (1 Cor 2:11), and further, "the natural man

---

[1] See Roger D. Haight, "Mission: The Symbol for Understanding the Church Today," earlier in this issue.

[2] *Ibid.*

does not accept what is taught by the Spirit of God. For him, that is absurdity" (1 Cor 2:14). This absurdity culminated in Christ's cross, and
a sign of God's love must also manifest that paradox. This is not to deny
that the Church must listen to the signs of the times, such as the demand
for experiential criteria of authenticity and for relevance for life in this
world, but ultimately it must develop criteria from its own resources of
faith for its mission.[3]

Thus, to take as criterion for the Church whether or not it is effectively
manifesting God's love, far from simplifying the question "Why the
Church?", actually confronts us with a further difficult question: What is
the nature of God's love that the Church is to signify? The response of
this article to that question makes the Church as worshiping community
more central than an explanation which makes outward mission primary.[4]

Thus this article attempts to respond to the question of the Church by
reflecting on its ground in Trinitarian love. Part 1 will consider the
problem as it arises out of the ambiguity of love. That will move me in
Part 2 to consider the cross of Christ as central to understanding God's
love, and to develop principles from that center for interpreting God's
love in social-religious development. In Part 3 I will apply those principles to an understanding of the Church today, and present some
reflections on its call to transformation.

THE AMBIGUITIES OF LOVE

The usual argument for the presence of grace outside the Church,
which seems to make the Church important mainly as an articulation of
what is happening everywhere, is the presence in the world of unconditional self-sacrificing love. The ground of this possibility is the gift of
Christ to the world as the "supernatural existential" of our present
human situation. The basic presupposition of "anonymous Christianity"
is that human spirit involves an "unlimited openness for the limitless
being of God," and that *de facto* we live in a world called to God through
the final gift of Christ to the world.[5] Thus Rahner can say: "If a man
accepts the revelation, he posits by that fact the act of supernatural

---

[3] Richard McBrien advocates this need for the Church to change out of its own
self-understanding through "the way of self-determination"; see his *The Remaking of the
Church: An Agenda for Reform* (New York, 1973), p. 80. His concern is more for structural
reform, however, whereas my article questions the very ground of the Church, which
ultimately must guide such restructuring.

[4] Haight's article presents the community aspect of the Church as "relative" to its
primary function of mission. The position of my article will be that community is equally
primary with mission, each presupposing the other.

[5] Karl Rahner, "Anonymous Christians," *Theological Investigations* 6 (New York, 1974)
392.

faith. But he also already accepts this revelation whenever he really accepts *himself* completely, for it already speaks *in* him."[6] Not only is true self-acceptance within immediate transcendence of conscious knowing and doing thus seen as grounded in grace and an implicit act of supernatural faith, but also whenever an act of authentic love of neighbor is performed it must have as ground supernatural love of God, whether this is explicitly known or not. Rahner says in another place:

Above all, most theologians today would still shrink from the proposition which gives our fundamental thesis its ultimate meaning, its real clarity and inescapable character, viz., that wherever a genuine love of man attains its proper nature and its moral absoluteness and depth, it is in addition always so underpinned and heightened by God's saving grace that it is also love of God, whether it be explicitly considered to be such a love by the subject or not.[7]

Since 1965, when Rahner wrote that article, it is no longer true that "most theologians today would still shrink" from such a proposition. Rather, it seems commonly presupposed. Thus, in his *Method in Theology* Lonergan speaks of religious conversion as a state of being in love unconditionally. Such a consciousness can dispense with positive theology, for its love is "oriented positively to what is transcendent in lovableness." He comments:

It may be objected that *nihil amatum nisi praecognitum*. But while that is true of other human love, it need not be true of the love with which God floods our hearts through the Holy Spirit he has given us (Rom 5:5). That grace could be the finding that grounds our seeking God through natural reason and through positive religion. It could be the touchstone by which we judge whether it is really God that natural reason reaches or positive religion preaches. It could be the grace that God offers all men, that underpins what is good in the religions of mankind, that explains how those that never heard the gospel can be saved.[8]

Heribert Mühlen has argued to a similar position from the nature of a love that truly responds to another as other. If one is truly acting out of self-surrendering love in responding to another, that person must be grounded in the "unlimited Thou" of God, since one's own particularity cannot ground our surrender beyond ourselves nor can the particularity of the other.[9] Thus the affirmation of *Lumen gentium* that "everlasting salvation" can be attained by those who "do not know the gospel of Christ or his Church, yet sincerely seek God" (no. 16) is given content by

[6] *Ibid.*, p. 394.

[7] Karl Rahner, "Reflections on the Unity of the Love of Neighbor and the Love of God," *Theological Investigations* 6 (New York, 1974) 237.

[8] Bernard J. F. Lonergan, S.J., *Method in Theology* (London, 1972) p. 278.

[9] Heribert Mühlen, *Die abendländische Seinsfrage als der Tod Gottes und der Aufgang einer neuen Gotteserfahrung* (Paderborn, 1968) pp. 55–56.

these theologians as referring to those who manifest in their lives "self-transcending" love of God and neighbor.[10]

These theological arguments seem solid and convincing for the possibility and actuality of self-transcending love outside the Church. They are less helpful, however, for specifying where in fact such love is actually present and what conditions are needed for its full working out. In the first place, with the exception of Mühlen, their principles are derived primarily from the self-transcending subject, with less attention to the interrelationship of such subjects, so that the social dimension does not come clearly into view. The Church, however, as a social institution, requires criteria derived from social development.[11] In the second place, their criteria are not clearly experiential or verifiable, because they do not focus sufficiently on committed love over a long period of time with its stages of development. Metaphysical principles are essential, but without the further experiential criteria there is little clarity for determining what ought to be done. Experience shows that the initial experience of love is no firm criterion; for the dark side very soon appears with its jealousies, angers, and destructive drives. As one Jungian analyst put it, "love is more complex than its emotions, just as God is mystery, not enthusiasms."[12] In the deeper regions of the human person, even our most "altruistic" intentions often prove to be efforts to see ourselves as valuable, and the fidelity of our commitment is shaken by lack of response in the other. A depth analyst such as Freud concluded toward the end of his life that some blocks to that freedom which is the basis of *any* true love are all but insurmountable, and that the drive to self-destruction is all but irresistible.[13] Experiential criteria for love thus have to take fidelity in time into consideration, a fidelity to the initial vision that may seem impossible in face of the "realism" of daily life.[14]

[10] As is clear from their arguments, "self-transcending" has different meanings in the theologians cited according to their total theological viewpoint. They hold in common, however, that such "self-transcendence" indicates the action of God's grace.

[11] Lonergan's analysis of intersubjectivity (see *Method in Theology*, pp. 55 ff.) and of cognitive, constitutive, and effective meaning which constitutes the Church as society (pp. 362 f.) provides helpful principles for such a social-developmental analysis, but they are sketchy and need fleshing out. Paul Tillich, also, in Vol. 3 of his *Systematic Theology* analyzes Christian spiritual community in the context of world history (3 vols. in one; Chicago, 1967, esp. pp. 382–93). His treatments of historical "self-integration," "self-creativity," and "self-transcendence" have some similarity to the second, third, and fourth stages of my analysis (see below). They are not, however, interrelated by Tillich in a developmental way.

[12] See James Hillman, *Insearch: Psychology and Religion* (New York, 1967) p. 82.

[13] Sigmund Freud, "Analysis Terminable and Interminable," *Standard Edition*, ed. James Strachey (London: Hogarth) 23 (1964) 252.

[14] In his classic book on love, Vladimir Solovyev makes this very point. The keen emotion of love glimpses a transcendent reality, but it comes and passes away. What remains is

Not only does experience show selfless love to be ambiguous and difficult in our individual lives; it is even more clearly challenged in our efforts to bring about just social structures. As John C. Bennett commented in a not outdated article,

Enthusiasm for a cause is not enough. There is a phase in a particular struggle when the cause may simplify one's life, make decisions clear, enable one to know with whom to stand. But complexities finally overtake such simplifications. One discovers there are no total solutions, that even successes create new and unanticipated problems, that actual alternatives call for new and troublesome decisions. Those who have been most political and activistic often find the people with whom they have worked split away over strategies and develop a shocking hostility toward one another. . . . [15]

A similar conclusion about the difficulty, if not impossibility, of establishing a socially-just world order was reached by Reinhold Niebuhr. After studying the historical evidence at length, he concluded that whereas individual selfless love is difficult enough, institutional selfless love is proven historically to be highly unlikely, if not impossible. "The selfishness of human communities must be regarded as an inevitability. Where it is inordinate it can be checked only by competing assertions of interest; and these can be effective only if coercive methods are added to moral and rational persuasion."[16] He concludes that the moral obtuseness and self-interest of human collectives make a morality of pure disinterestedness impossible, so that any overly optimistic expectation of it must come to terms with a history that evidences the contrary.

There are signs of a growing optimism that perhaps social change can be brought about if there is Christian community, but even those attempts point to the difficulty of following through with such communities. An editor of the *Post American*, a periodical published by a radical social-action group in Chicago, put it thus:

The experience of our own small community in Chicago, however, is probably far too typical of what has happened with many. We watched helplessly with bewilderment and disillusionment as all our highest dreams and noblest efforts to build community crumbled around us. There were many reasons for this: our lack of wisdom in handling interpersonal friction, a fear of authority, a pride that often kept us from learning from others. As we look back, perhaps the biggest reason is that we simply did not understand the centrality of the Spirit to

---

faith in love that stands firm to the end despite the cross. "In our materialistic society," he writes, "it is impossible to preserve genuine love, unless we understand and accept it as a moral achievement" (*The Meaning of Love* [New York, 1947] p. 67).

[15] John C. Bennett, "Two Christianities," *Worldview*, October 1973, p. 24.

[16] Reinhold Niebuhr, *Moral Man and Immoral Society* (New York, 1960 [first publ. 1932]) p. 272.

building community; now our greatest hopes in rebuilding stem from the beginnings of an "unclogging" of the Spirit among us.[17]

A similar conclusion was reached by Rev. Leo Mahon in his work in an experimental parish in San Miguelito, Panama. When he went there in 1963, he organized a group of 500 men, using methods learned under Saul Alinsky in Chicago. This group disintegrated almost immediately. He realized that what was needed was a "new man" and began to evangelize the people and to seek conversion of life.[18] He learned that what obstructs social change and community-building is deeper than mere good intentions can eradicate; in fact, what seemed needed was both personal and social conversion to Christ.

This imposing body of evidence cautions us against concluding too quickly from theological possibility to the actual working out of selfless love within or outside the Church. It also points to the necessity of developing theological criteria of its presence that include more explicitly the social dimension and the experiential dimension that includes fidelity in time. I turn now to this task.

TRINITARIAN LOVE AS REVEALED IN CHRIST'S CROSS

Since as Christians we hold the centrality of Christ for revealing God's love, I propose to examine how Scripture presents his life as foundation for our theological criteria. What has emerged from recent studies is the centrality of Christ's death/resurrection, not only for interpreting his own life and that of Christians, but also for interpreting the self-giving love of the Trinity. That Christ's death and resurrection was central to the Christian message has become clear from Scripture studies. The core of the early Church kerygma was "that Christ died for our sins in accordance with the Scriptures, that he was buried, that he was raised on the third day . . . and that he appeared to Cephas, then to the Twelve" (1 Cor 15:3-5).[19] This was the key event in whose light all the other events of Christ's life were interpreted by the Evangelists.[20] Not only

[17] Jim Wallis and Robert Sabath, "The Spirit in the Church," *Post American*, February 1975, pp. 4–5.

[18] See the unpublished dissertation by Robert J. Delaney, *Pastoral Renewal in a Local Church: Investigation of the Pastoral Principles Involved in the Development of the Local Church in San Miguelito, Panama* (Münster, 1973) esp. pp. 91–92.

[19] See Joseph A. Fitzmyer, "Pauline Theology," *Jerome Biblical Commentary* (Englewood Cliffs, N.J., 1968) pp. 812 f., for further development of the centrality of the cross in Paul's theology. Norman Perrin develops this point in Mark's Gospel, the earliest of the Synoptics, in his *The New Testament: An Introduction* (New York, 1974) p. 148.

[20] Hans Urs von Balthasar develops this point in his extended article on the paschal mystery, "Mysterium paschale," in *Mysterium salutis* 3/2 (Cologne, 1969) pp. 133 ff. Christian Schütz makes the same point in his interpretation of the Gospel miracles in the

Christ's life but Christian life was interpreted in the light of the paschal mystery. Thus, the description of the Christian life in all three Synoptics[21] is put after the prediction of the Passion, when Jesus turned specifically to teach his disciples. The call to become as little children, to forgive unconditionally, to exercise authority by serving, to remain faithful in marriage, etc., are all seen in the light of the coming Passion. John continues this view and calls the faithful to love one another as Jesus loved them (Jn 13:34), saying that the greatest love was "that a man lay down his life for his friends" (Jn 15:12).

To see Christ's cross and resurrection as central for interpreting his life and the life of Christian discipleship is not novel. What is relatively recent is to see in it a revelation of Trinitarian love. A tradition of interpreting God's being as perfect act and absolutely immutable made it difficult to see Christ's suffering as revealing anything about the Father's self-sacrificing love, to say nothing of the Son's divine personhood.[22] Thus Hans Urs von Balthasar was developing unfamiliar ideas when he wrote in his recent major article on the paschal mystery:

God's emptying (in the Incarnation) is ontically made possible by God's eternal emptying, His threefold personal self-gift. Consequently, even the created person is not primarily to be described as "standing in oneself," but more deeply (if the person is created in God's image and likeness) as "returning to oneself (*reflexio completa*) from being centered outside," and as "standing outside oneself as self-giving and responding interior."[23]

Balthasar thus interprets God's own Triune love from the self-emptying love of Christ revealed in his incarnation/death/resurrection.

Heribert Mühlen has taken up this theme in developing his interper-

---

light of Christ's death/resurrection; see his "Die Mysterien des öffentlichen Lebens und Wirkens Jesu," *ibid.*, esp. pp. 119–23.

[21] Mk 10:32–45; Mt 17:22–18:35; Lk 9:51 ff. Paul J. Achtemeier develops this point at length in his recent commentary on Mark (*Mark*, ed. Gerhard Krodel [Philadelphia, 1975] pp. 96–100). William G. Thompson makes the point for Matthew's Gospel by pointing out the interspersing of the Passion predictions with advice to the community (*Matthew's Advice to a Divided Community: Mt 17,22—18, 35* [Rome, 1970] pp. 14 ff.). Luke places his advice in the context of the "journey to Jerusalem."

[22] Heribert Mühlen presents the patristic arguments against the Father suffering, arguments which in post-Chalcedonian theology also spoke against the divine Son suffering; see his *Die Veränderlichkeit Gottes als Horizont einer zukünftigen Christologie* (Münster, 1969) pp. 16–20. There have been sporadic affirmations since then of the Father's suffering (Luther's paradoxical theology was one such example), but they have not been widespread till recently. One recent study out of the Lutheran tradition is Kazoh Kitamori, *Theology of the Pain of God* (Richmond, 1965 [originally 1958]). Jürgen Moltmann has also addressed this theme; see his *The Crucified God: The Cross of Christ as the Foundation and Criticism of Christian Theology* (London, 1974).

[23] Balthasar, "Mysterium paschale," pp. 147–48 (my translation).

sonal view of Trinitarian love.[24] He sees in the Son's giving Himself up (Eph 5:2.25; Gal 2:20) a revelation of the Father's own "not sparing His own son" (Rom 8:32) and handing Him over for us (Jn 3:16). The cross reveals the high point both of the Father's not sparing His own and the Son's not sparing Himself, and the moment of their unity in giving is the moment of the sending of the Spirit (Jn 19:30). Thus Mühlen sees the Spirit as the expression in person of the Father's and Son's joint self-giving love, who in turn effects self-giving community among those He is "sent" to. "The being (einai) of God," Mühlen writes, "the essence of His essence, is the giving away of His own."[25] Being the fulness of manifestation of God's Spirit, the cross is not seen as a single act but the culmination of a life of self-giving and the fruitfulness of this life in community formation.

This theological view of the paschal mystery as revealing God's own Trinitarian love places that event in the larger context of all God's loving action in salvation history as the culmination of His sovereignly-free absolute fidelity to His covenantal promise to Israel, a promise that not even Israel's infidelity could block. Mühlen expresses well this mysterious fidelity of God:

In his convenantal conduct God is the absolutely unchangeable newness of His freedom, and this does not exclude the fact that He reacts sovereignly to what man does. . . . The death of the Son of God, who is the revelation of the

---

[24] Mühlen, "Veränderlichkeit Gottes," pp. 30–34. Methodologically, it is important to note the difference between von Balthasar and Mühlen and, say, Rahner. All three have constitutive Christologies (see Schineller, "Christ and the Church: A Spectrum of Understandings," earlier in this issue, for a description of this type), but von Balthasar and Mühlen have an interpersonal ontology behind their positions, as distinguished from what Mühlen would term a "transcendental subject" view that sees being as the horizon of one's personal "being-in-the-world" (as Rahner, similar to Heidegger). An interpersonal ontology focuses on interpersonal communication as primary revelation of being, so that one views being as a sort of union of opposites, and the Trinitarian perspective comes clearly into view. The cross is then interpreted as dying to autonomous personhood for the sake of emerging communal being, and emphasis moves from individual spiritual growth to community growth. It is clear how community and Church are more essential in this view than with a more subject-centered ontology. Such an interpersonal ontology is an underlying presupposition of my article.

[25] Ibid., p. 31 (my translation). This is a further development of Mühlen's basic position that the best analogy for the Holy Spirit is "we" in person. The Father is initiating ground, analogous to "I" in interpersonal relationships. The Son is coequal respondent, analogous to "thou", joined in "mutual" love with the Father. And the Spirit springs from their "joint" love, the expression of their union in love while maintaining their otherness. (See his Der Heilige Geist als Person [Münster, 1963] pp. 100–169 for a full development of this position.) Thus the action of the Spirit in our hearts, in this view, is to bring about the same sort of joint self-giving while maintaining our differences. The Spirit is community-forming.

omnipotence of God in the impotence of the cross, is the completely unexpected expression of the free fidelity of God to His promises, which is incapable of being grasped by any sort of a priori schema.[26]

It is this larger salvation-historical context that enables us to derive from Christ's cross/resurrection both transcendental qualities of God's Trinitarian love and experiential historical stages of religious social development. The next three sections unfold these implications.

Qualities of Trinitarian Love Revealed in Cross/Resurrection

If we view the cross/resurrection event as revealing God's Trinitarian love, four qualities of that love appear: His sovereign freedom, His fidelity to His promises and the continuity of His call, the universality of His love, and its community-forming power. His freedom is revealed because the cross shows that no other power, whether human evil or demonic, can stand against God's free self-gift. His fidelity appears in the cross as God's standing by His covenant despite Israel's rejection of it. His universal love is revealed because through the cross God's love breaks through narrow national boundaries and extends salvation to all, Jew and Gentile alike. Finally, through Christ's dying and rising God frees the world from its alienation in order to produce a new people through the sending of the Spirit. I will consider each of these in turn.

First, God's sovereign freedom is revealed in His determination to give Himself despite the rejection of His people. The cross shows God's love as not conditioned on whether or not it is reciprocated, but as itself the ground of our ability to reciprocate. It is the sort of love to which Matthew calls Jesus' disciples: "If you love those who love you, what reward have you?" (Mt 5:46).[27] It is this love's sovereign freedom from outside influence that grounds Paul's conviction that since God did not spare His own Son but gave Him up on our behalf (Rom 8:32), then no power, neither life nor death, neither angel nor principality, can separate us from God's love in Christ Jesus (Rom 8:38–39). The ground of this "freedom from" is God's total self-possession and sovereign power to commit Himself *for* some end. His absolute initiative is the source of the unconditional covenant promised to David[28] and realized in the "yes" of Christ to God's promises (2 Cor 1:20). Thus God's sovereign freedom from inner-world dependency is not mere arbitrariness, as seems implied in nominalism, but is precisely the ground of His absolute covenant fidelity.

[26] *Ibid.*, pp. 29–30 (my translation).
[27] Matthew says this in the context of calling the disciples to love their enemies (Mt 5:44) and ultimately to "be perfect, as your heavenly Father is perfect" (5:48).
[28] See Delbert R. Hillers, *Covenant: The History of a Biblical Idea* (Baltimore, 1969) pp. 98–119.

Secondly, implied in God's sovereign freedom, therefore, is His fidelity and the continuity of His self gift to humanity. The cross is the paradoxical revelation that God's fidelity is able to accept the freedom of His people even to reject Him and His Son and still not take back His unconditional offer of love. Israel had the background for understanding this in its theology of covenant. The Sinai covenant was conditioned on their fidelity to the divine commandments, and since Israel proved unfaithful, the later prophets pronounced that covenant broken[29] and interpreted her national trials (destruction of Jerusalem, exile, dispersion) as the consequences of this breach of covenant.[30] Despite all this, God's plan of the covenant remained unchanged. God would renew the covenant of Sinai (Ez 16:60) and that of David (Ez 34:23 f), and would change their hearts by the gift of the divine Spirit (Ez 36:26 ff.), so that they would again be His people. This unconditional fidelity of God, which regathers Israel despite her dispersion through infidelity, is thus brought to surprising revelation in the cross/resurrection event, where Christ's words of forgiveness as seen by Luke (23:34) reveal the ultimate in God's willingness to forgive and reunite despite all.[31]

Thirdly, the cross thus reveals God's love as universally open. It is Christ's death for our sin that Paul sees as God's offer of reconciliation to the whole world (2 Cor 5:18) through repentance and forgiveness of sin. Christ healed the division between Jew and Gentile in his own flesh, according to the author of Ephesians (2:14–15), and prepares in himself the ground of reunification. In principle no one, including enemies, is excluded from the call to "be reconciled to God," though the call may in fact be refused, at least in Matthew's view, and the judgment will consist in whether or not one has opened in hospitality to "his least disciples" (Mt 25:31–46). It is important not to separate the universality of God's offer of love from its realization on the cross. In Matthew the cross is the bridge to universalism; in Luke, though universalism is present in intent from the beginning, it is realized only through the cross/resurrection and sending of the Spirit.[32] Thus the particularism of Jesus' mission during his life is finally broken through only after his death/resurrection. That

---

[29] See Jer 22:9; 31:32; Hos 2:4; Ez 16:15–43, etc.

[30] See "Covenant" in *Dictionary of Biblical Theology*, rev. ed. by Xavier Leon-Dufour (New York, 1973) p. 96.

[31] It is such trust in God's faithful love that grounds Paul's mission to preach the kerygma of reconciliation (2 Cor 5:20–21) and is behind Matthew's instructions to forgive unconditionally (Mt 18:21–22) even when someone else has the grievance (Mt 5:23–24). According to John, Jesus' postresurrection gift to the disciples was the Spirit that empowered them to forgive (Jn 20:23).

[32] See Eugene A. LaVerdiere and William G. Thompson, "New Testament Communities in Transition: A Study of Matthew and Luke," earlier in this issue.

breakthrough was precisely the extension of the call to become God's people in Christ beyond the limitations of Judaism.

Thus, finally, the cross/resurrection event reveals God's love as community-forming through the "sending" of His Spirit. It grounds what Paul calls a "new creation" (2 Cor 5:17), or a "new covenant" in the Spirit (2 Cor 3:6–13), which is celebrated in the Eucharist as the covenant ratified in the blood of Christ and recalling his death until he comes (1 Cor 11:25 f.). Luke portrays the very event of Pentecost as a new Sinai epiphany, the Spirit covenant fulfilling the covenant of the law.[33] Not only were the disciples empowered by the Spirit to witness, but believers were brought together in common worship and shared all things in common (Acts 2:44).[34] John's view is similar, though the Spirit is not as clearly linked to the community formation. He clearly links the sending of the Spirit to Jesus' death/resurrection (Jn 7:39; 16:7; 19:30), and he also sees Jesus' death as a sort of seed giving rise to a new community (Jn 12:24). When the Spirit is given He is a power for reconciliation (Jn 20:23), so that the disciples might lead the lost back to unity. Thus the very witness of the disciples is to be their communion and love for one another (Jn 13:35), and their unity is to reveal God's own unity (Jn 17:20–21). In some mysterious way, therefore, Christ's dying in submission to the Father's will is seen in these accounts as an event through which God builds a new covenant community through the sending of the Spirit. His action throughout history of calling a people to Himself is brought to fulfilment (in principle, if not in time) through establishing a new people by His Spirit.[35]

These four qualities of God's Trinitarian love—its grounding in God's sovereign freedom and fidelity, its universal intent and community-forming power—are manifested historically most fully in the cross/resurrection event, but they are transcendent and present analogously in every stage of salvation history. The Church, as we shall see, embodies not simply the final and fullest stage of divine action, but includes the forms characteristic of preceding stages as well. Thus experiential criteria to identify the prevailing stage of religious development must

[33] See Thierry Maertens, O.S.A., *A Feast in Honor of Yahweh* (Notre Dame, 1965) pp. 148–51.

[34] See LaVerdiere and Thompson, *art. cit.*

[35] Throughout Israel's history the Spirit of Yahweh serves His covenant people. It inspires leaders at critical moments (Gideon, Jg 6:34; Samson, Jg 13:25; Saul, 1 S 10:6, etc.) all "in service of the establishment of the Kingdom of God in Israel" (Walter Eichrodt, *Theology of the Old Testament* 2, 51). Later the Spirit is manifested more personally through anointing prophets with Yahweh's "Word" to call Israel back to the covenant, and still later as the inner power that will establish Yahweh's law in their hearts (Ez 36:26 ff.); *ibid.*, pp. 57–65. Thus the Pentecost experience is situated in a history of progressive personalizing and interiorizing of Yahweh's Spirit in service of His covenant people.

also be developed in order to guide the Church to fuller growth. Hence I turn now to the question of social-religious development.

Notion of Historical Development as Help to Understanding Church

Wherever it is manifest, God's love will show the qualities both of sovereign freedom and of fidelity in forming community of an ever more universal character. These qualities, however, will show up differently in the Noah covenant than in that of Moses or the New Promise. Because of God's fidelity, each of these covenant promises will be included in the succeeding ones, but each succeeding covenant will also reveal an element of newness that comes from the sovereign freedom of God's love.[36] This paradox of God's freedom and fidelity, of prophetic challenge and continuity of commitment, confronts us inevitably with the question whether or not there are stages of historical development that enter into succeeding stages as necessary presuppositions for their emergence. In other words, is there a law of historical development that will help us to interpret the role of the Church today?

A springboard into this difficult question is given by Mühlen in his treatment of a theology of politics in *Entsakralisierung*.[37] He observes that a certain view of updating as simply a matter of ridding the Church of Old Testament forms and introducing "religionless religion" is overly simplistic. The Old Testament is not some fixed quantity that lies behind us so that we are in an entirely new order. It is an eternal, enduring covenant that must be realized in history ever again. This means that the Old Testament can never be a reality of the past that we have outgrown. "It belongs, therefore, to the 'essence' of the New Covenant that the Old as having been still is present, for the newness of the New Covenant even today can only come into appearance in the tension of the Old Covenant promise."[38] On this basis the Spirit of the New Covenant does not simply replace the law of the Old, but in some sense contains it while surpassing it. Behind such a view is a notion of development that needs closer examination.

This notion of development appears most clearly in human development but is verified in every new stage of evolution. Thus, as Teilhard de Chardin has shown, each successive stage of evolution includes yet transcends the previous stage, molecules being contained in living cells, cells included in sensate life, sense included in human life, and so on.

---

[36] This would imply both continuity and divine intervention, using the categories of J. Patout Burns, "The Economy of Salvation in Patristic Theology," earlier in this issue. I shall develop this more at length later.

[37] Heribert Mühlen, *Entsakralisierung: Ein epochales Schlagwort in seiner Bedeutung für die Zukunft der christlichen Kirchen* (Paderborn, 1971) pp. 177–85.

[38] *Ibid.*, p. 178 (my translation).

What appears in evolution as a whole, Erik Erikson has shown in human development through the various crises of trust/mistrust, initiative/guilt, identity/diffusion, etc.[39] Each stage enters into the successful working out of the succeeding stage or else introduces a deviation that prevents a full working out of the process. Lonergan articulates this notion of development in connection with the three types of conversion (intellectual, moral, and religious) he sees in self-transcending consciousness.

Because intellectual, moral, and religious conversions all have to do with self-transcendence, it is possible, when all three occur within a single consciousness, to conceive their relations in terms of sublation. I would use this notion in Karl Rahner's sense rather than Hegel's to mean that what sublates goes beyond what is sublated, introduces something new and distinct, puts everything on a new basis, yet so far from interfering with the sublated or destroying it, on the contrary needs it, includes it, preserves all its proper features and properties, and carries them forward to a fuller realization within a richer context.[40]

The key point in this view is that previous stages are not destroyed but even raised to higher realization in their own right, while being integrated in the richer context. Thus, sensation in humans is richer than in animals, and cells in animals are more complex than those in plant life, etc. Lonergan finds this phenomenon in the stages of conversions: the intellectual conversion from conceptualism to judgments of reality is contained in the moral conversion to value choices on the basis of the objective good, and both are contained in the religious conversion to the principle of unlimited love. If this is true of individual consciousness, which analysis can show presupposes an interpersonal context in order to develop,[41] it seems reasonable to expect that it is also true analogously of social-religious consciousness, such that stages of development could be seen as preparatory for the Church of Christ springing from the cross/resurrection event.

To discover such stages in Scripture, however, presents a difficult methodological question. There are multiple theologies in both Old and New Testaments[42] and it is impossible simply to take one of these as speaking for the whole of Scripture. On the other hand, the systematic theologian does not merely take over scriptural theologies; he develops

[39] Erik H. Erikson, *Identity, Youth, and Crisis* (New York, 1968) chap. 3, "The Life Cycle: Epigenesis of Identity," pp. 91–141.

[40] Lonergan, *Method in Theology*, p. 241.

[41] Erikson's stages, e.g., are all socially conditioned. One cannot grow in trust without a trustworthy environment, etc. Language itself, the product of social culture, conditions personal growth, and love is the necessary environment for growth. Thus person is essentially interpersonal, and one could expect that the individual person's stages of growth imply social stages. Analysis will have to show whether this is true.

[42] See LaVerdiere and Thompson, *art. cit.*, as but one example.

categories suitable for modern problems and attempts to correlate these with the data of Scripture. Since the Church is a historical reality, it does demand historical analysis (the problem cannot simply be bypassed); and if this analysis is to produce more than historical relativity, some foundation in laws of development seems called for. Since, further, the Church is not merely a sociological reality but a mystery of God's grace and hence a spiritual-social reality, we will look to spiritual psychology to work out a paradigm of the stages of spiritual development (presupposing these reveal stages of social development as well) and then correlate this paradigm with Scripture to show how it corresponds to major stages in Judeo-Christian history.[43]

The first stage of spiritual growth is to lay the foundation of an integrated personality through relationships with parents, peers, and members of the other sex, as well as the discipline of rules, in order to consolidate one's self-possession and personal freedom sufficiently to sustain constructively the break-through of spiritual experience. At this level one interiorizes collective norms of one's parents or one's environment—what Freud would call the "superego"—in order to bring one's self-centered desires into integration with social expectations and the rights of others. The personality is fed and strengthened through these close relationships and rules and opened to a broader social participation. I will call this the "familial" stage. It is characterized by close (even blood) relationships to members of one's religious group and by emphasis on obedience to law. God is known more externally, as an authority figure and lawgiver, and one identifies oneself primarily in terms of social expectations. It is an essential stage of self-integration; otherwise spiritual experience can break the tenuous integration or be distorted because of the one-sidedness of personal development.[44]

[43] "Paradigm" is used here in basically the same sense as in LaVerdiere and Thompson, *art. cit.*, to mean what "*in*-forms and *in*-fluences the life of the community and its members." There, however, Scripture is the source of the paradigm, and the present day makes it its own. Here the paradigm is worked out from present-day developments in spiritual psychology with an eye to its correlation with Scripture. Here, also, its implications are worked out systematically as an aid to interpreting scriptural data developmentally. It may well be that further study would show that this is what exegetes also do (judging from cultural trends in exegesis), without fully articulating the present-day thought-frame being used. This could be a question for further investigation.

[44] It is difficult to give in detail all the sources of evidence for these stages. My own dissertation has provided much data by examining Freud, Jung, and Moreno in the light of Mühlen's theology of the Holy Spirit; see *Spirit: Divine and Human. The Theology of the Holy Spirit of Heribert Mühlen and Its Relevance for Evaluating the Data of Psychotherapy* (unpublished, Fordham University, 1974) pp. 378–477. Further evidence has come from a social interpretation of the *Spiritual Exercises* of St. Ignatius: human freedom is needed even to begin the *Exercises*, a spiritual break-through initiates the Second Week, it is integrated in one's life in the Election and Third Week, and moves to a missionary thrust in

Secondly, conscious integration of oneself in society necessarily involves a one-sidedness that leaves other aspects of one's individual uniqueness undeveloped and suppressed. At some time or other there is a break-through of "spiritual experience" springing from one's spiritual center—what has been called the "superconscious."[45] This center is beyond rationality, much as the subconscious is prerational. It is the dimension of the personality whence come intuitions, artistic inspiration, love, and personal experience of God.[46] Its emergence frees aspects of one's wholeness that have been denied consciousness by the effort at social integration—the "dark side" of one's personality, guilt, shame, mystery. Thus the transition to this dimension is disorienting to one's "normal" view of life. There is demanded a sort of "dying" of the conscious self in opening to this new transcendence, whether it is experienced in a "great love" or in more direct experience of God.[47] One's personal self is now not so much agent as respondent, and has to learn a new way of co-operating with the power and influence of this new dimension. The new centering experience frees one from collective relationships to the beginning of individuation, which at the same time opens one to the universality of the spirit. However, this is only the vision

---

the Fourth Week and *Contemplatio*. What I have found most helpful to describe the stages is the work of C. G. Jung (quite widely available) and his follower Roberto Assagioli. Thus, Jung found the distinction between personal self ("personal unconscious") and spiritual self ("collective unconscious") to be verified the world over and in every age. These are not separate; the personal self (or ego) is a particular reflection of one's total spiritual self that is developed as the ego stabilizes itself in the world. Jung saw this social stabilization of the ego as the work of the first half of life, till about age 35 to 40 (see "The Stages of Life," in *The Portable Jung*, ed. Joseph Campbell [New York, 1975] pp. 3–22). Spiritual experience could occur before this, but it could not develop fully unless the ego was thus strengthened. Erikson's stages in the life cycle would basically correspond to the work of this stage. Conflicts in this stage, according to Assagioli, "occur between the 'normal' drives, between these drives and the conscious ego, or between the ego and the outer world (particularly human beings closely related, such as parents, mate or children)" (*Psychosynthesis* [New York, 1971] p. 43).

[45] Assagioli gives a fine description of the indications preceding and accompanying this "spiritual awakening." The "ordinary man" may begin to experience a vague and elusive "lack," which may lead to intensified activity to escape the sense of meaninglessness. This might increase even to the extent of despairing of life itself. The break-through itself of the spiritual dimension opens one to an ecstatic experience of love and truth and a whole new generosity toward life (*Psychosynthesis*, pp. 40–46).

[46] A helpful article describing the spiritual dimension in a systematic way is Benedict M. Ashley, O.P., "A Psychological Model with a Spiritual Dimension," *Pastoral Psychology*, May 1972, pp. 31–40.

[47] Assagioli's description focuses more on the mystical aspects of this break-through, whereas "ecstatic love" itself shows many of the same qualities as the break-through of the self. It decenters the person and places one in a new interpersonal context that reveals its grounding in a transcendent Other. See Solovyev, *The Meaning of Love*, pp. 58 ff.

of universality, not yet its realization. In time, because one's relationships and ways of acting are still patterned on the old model, the experience ebbs, love cools, or one loses the vision of the spiritual and is left with a conscience sensitized by the experience but with the same old narrow self and guilt. In fear of this state, one may intensify efforts at purification, but this only deepens one in the previous self-structure and increases alienation.[48] Learning submission to transcendence is a long and difficult process.

Thus, thirdly, there is what might be called an "incarnational" stage of transforming one's relationships in line with one's experience of God and the new break-through of spiritual love. This stage is essentially communitarian, since one's relationships cannot be transformed apart from a community undergoing a similar transformation. This presupposes the freedom gained in the second stage, for only if one is centered and whole can relationships be true. Thus one continues to submit to the transcendent dimension in a growing and mutual submission to and unification with others. But also this stage presupposes and transforms the first stage by a growing decentering from oneself for the sake of the other through a sort of "ecstatic love" which does not annihilate one's self but brings increased self-understanding and self-gift in the new love.[49] The process involves a purification of one's previous self-centered feelings, understandings, and choices—a sort of "dark night" of the senses and spirit—which emerges into a deeper unification and indwelling in the other. St. John of the Cross expresses well the ecstatic nature of this love: "Wherefore the soul may know well if it loves God or no; for if it loves Him, it will have no heart for itself, but only for God."[50] Not only is this increasing other-centeredness true of relationship to God, but increasingly of all one's relationships in God.

Fourthly, as the person (and community) grows in "ecstatic self-gift" through a deepening dying to self-centeredness into greater unification in community through the transcendent love, one experiences a desire to communicate the joy one has found with others beyond the limits of the believing community. Thus St. Teresa and St. John of the Cross were led by their mystical purification to become active reformers. Perfect love, as

[48] See Assagioli, *Psychosynthesis*, pp. 46–49.

[49] John Cowburn develops the notion of "ecstatic love" in his *Love and the Person: A Philosophical Theory and a Theological Essay* (London, 1967). As he notes, Christian mysticism is distinct from Eastern mysticism on this point, in that Eastern mysticism brings a greater union with one's own greater self and ultimate annihilation of one's self in the One, whereas Christian mysticism preserves the otherness of God in the process of ecstatic unification (pp. 347–55). Thus our third stage diverges from Eastern mysticism, and the divergence continues in the fourth stage.

[50] St. John of the Cross, *Spiritual Canticle*, ed. E. Allison Peers (New York, 1961) exposition of stanza 9, n. 4, p. 83. This passage is quoted in Cowburn, *op. cit.*, p. 345.

Richard of St. Victor noted, wants to share its beloved with others.[51] There is a "release of power," in the words of Rosemary Haughton, that springs from conversion to Christ in a loving community.[52] This fourth-stage person, grounded in the love of community and of Christ, desires to bring this communal love to those who still have not experienced it, and to do so freely, because one's need for love is fulfilled through the community. The creativity of the transcendent ground of God's communitarian love is thus freed to go out.[53]

These are four stages of spiritual growth into transformation by Trinitarian love. They are not independent of one another, but related in a logic of development. Familial relationships and rules bring developing integration and liberation of one's individual freedom. Grace touches that center of freedom and opens the self ecstatically to God and spiritual love.[54] As one integrates this spiritual dimension in free and freeing relationships to God and others, the liberation of self in this communal sharing breaks out in a transcendent desire to give freely the love one has experienced. Not only are the stages interdependent; successive stages preserve and develop more richly what was begun in previous stages. Individuation permits greater unification and deeper relations with others; ecstatic communal love effects deeper self-possession; finally, the stage of outgoing love increases one's delight in communal sharing, for that sharing is then not self-enclosed but creative of expanding love.[55] As with other developmental processes, break-throughs can take place in later stages before the previous ones are well developed, but they cannot normally continue in a solid way unless the presupposed stages are healed. Thus these stages form a sort of social-religious law of development akin to the other examples of development I have presented. It remains to see whether these stages cast light on and are correlated to the biblical data.

---

[51] *De trin.* 3, 11. Critical text and notes by Jean Ribaillier (Paris, 1958) p. 146. Ewert Cousins analyzes Richard's argument in "A Theology of Interpersonal Relations," *Thought* 45 (1970) 56–82.

[52] Rosemary Haughton, *The Transformation of Man: A Study of Conversion and Community* (New York, 1967) pp. 116–50.

[53] This correlates well with Mühlen's view of the Holy Spirit as breathed forth from the joint ecstatic love of Father and Christ at the moment of Christ's death. Gratuitous self-giving, in this view, springs from the joy of shared love. See n. 25 above.

[54] This is a moment of divine intervention that is not simply a further development of its preconditioning stage. See J. Patout Burns, *art. cit.*, for the distinction between a developmental and a condition-intervention schema of Gregory of Nyssa and Augustine respectively.

[55] The effect of succeeding stages on the preceding seems more an aspect of development, since it presupposes that each stage builds on the preceding and helps it unfold; see Burns, *art. cit.*

Correlation of Stages of Development with Biblical Data

The difficulty of such a correlation was mentioned before. An exegete could ground such stages variously: according to the various covenants, or particular persons such as Abraham and Moses, or various authors and traditions such as the Yahwist or Priestly account. I have chosen not simply to work from those positions but to sketch out a paradigm of spiritual development and to correlate it with what Scripture presents as major stages of Israel's development, both to elaborate our paradigm and to give further understanding to the biblical data. The stages were chosen with an eye to that correlation, so it should not be surprising to find how well they do fit.[56]

Thus, in the first place, we have a religious community of Israel, formed on the basis of the call and promise to Abraham, and the covenant and law given to Moses. The people were to be Abraham's offspring, so that membership depended for the most part (with the exception of converts) on blood relationship. These prepersonal bonds affected even the conferral of guilt and blessing—to the fourth or thousandth generation respectively (Dt 5:9 f.). The norm of conduct was provided by the Mosaic law, and this covenant presupposed and was conditioned by the people's observance of the law. Yahweh is seen as "Israel's God," not yet clearly as the "only God." He is transcendent in holiness, so that even Moses, the chosen one, could only look on the back of Yahweh lest he die (Ex 33:18–23). To represent Yahweh's "otherness," the priests wore special dress, and the Temple—a place "cut out" for Yahweh's worship—was His special place of presence. This corresponds almost exactly with the familial stage of religious development with its collective aspects of law and biological bonds of membership, and the transcendent otherness of Yahweh's Lordship. However, reflection will show that we each recapitulate that history in our own religious growth. If absolutized, this stage narrows in on itself in differentiating itself from others. It becomes judgmental and moralistic, and because outsiders are excluded it falls prey to one-sidedness. Although it is a necessary stage of growth, it must give way—through a sort of dying and rising—to a more personal and universal stage if it is not to harden in exclusiveness.

The second stage seems to have occurred with the destruction of Jerusalem and the dispersion. Secure symbols of identification such as the Temple and Jerusalem were destroyed and intense disorientation and despair resulted. A broader, more universal view of Yahweh's power and action emerged from the dispersed situation, so that this seems a decisive new stage in Israel's development. Fundamental to this stage were the prophecies that the old conditional covenant was abrogated

---

[56] See n. 43 above, for the meaning here of paradigm.

because of Israel's infidelity (Jer 31:21 etc.) and that Yahweh Himself would intervene and put His own Spirit in their hearts and make them keep the law and be His people (Ez 36:27). This break-through of Yahweh's transcendent unconditional love seems to have broadened their vision of Him from "Israel's God" to universal creator and "only God." Pagan gods are seen as nothing at all, and the Priestly creation account sees Yahweh as universal creator and Lord. Further, there is a move from collective guilt to individual responsibility, as seen in Ezechiel's admonitions to each Israelite (Ez 18). Correspondingly, there is a wider vision from narrow nationalism to seeing Jerusalem as eschatological center of world peace (Is 60:1–7).

This clearly corresponds to the stage of spiritual break-through with its polarity of individual responsibility and ecstatic universal visions. However, it is only the initial break-through, which sensitizes consciences, enlightens the intellect, and motivates to renewed activity; it is not the full transformation. The promises of inner transformation are all put in the future, and even though there is a growing closeness of relationship to Yahweh (seen especially in later wisdom literature), there is not yet the step to incarnating this spiritual dimension in human relationships that we find in the New Testament. In fact, in the ebbing of the Spirit, Israel increased its personal efforts toward purification and increased its laws and legalism.[57] A process of incarnating surrender to the spiritual dimension must take place if the people are not to stagnate between the spiritual break-through and their own efforts at self-salvation.

This third stage was inaugurated by Christ and brought to completed beginning in his death/resurrection. According to the Synoptics, Jesus not only experienced the personal break-through of relationship to the Father—as at his baptism—but also lived out in all life the implications of a Spirit-guided and empowered activity. This portrait corresponds well to what I have named the "incarnational" stage.[58] It involves a purification of one's own strategies and moral efforts for bringing about the good one envisions—such as we find in Christ's temptations—in

[57] Paul Ricoeur beautifully analyzes this process of increasing guilt with increasing attempts at self-purification; see *The Symbolism of Evil* (Boston, 1967) esp. pp. 126–47. The "Pharisee" is the "separated" man, alienated in his own efforts at purity (p. 137).

[58] Mühlen describes the change of spiritual experience from Old Testament to New at some length; see *Entsakralisierung*, pp. 264–320. He argues to a move from a transcendent, fearful experience of the sacred in the OT to an experience personalized and mediated by Christ and fellow Christians in the NT. See "Sacredness and Priesthood in a New Age," *Theology Digest* 21 (1973) 106–11, for a condensation of his position. My treatment relies heavily on his. My argument does not necessarily presuppose the historicity of the Scripture accounts. The writers' own attitudes toward Jesus reveal their spiritual experience.

order to submit one's powers freely to the Father's initiative. This purification of Jesus is linked to a deepened unification with the Father and an incipient spiritualization of social relationships. Thus Jesus is portrayed as using the intimate term "Abba" to express his relationship to the Father, a new sacred term reserved for the Father alone (Mt 23:9). And the Father is seen so close to him in John's Gospel that Jesus applies the Temple symbol to his own body (Jn 2:19-22) and exclaims to Philip that he who sees him sees the Father (Jn 14:9 ff.). Thus the fear of death that surrounded the epiphanies of Yahweh in our first stage is now transformed into an intimacy that involved Jesus' dying to himself in surrender to the Father's will. This decentering and unification increased till its culmination in the cross/resurrection event that John sees as the moment of "handing over" his Spirit (Jn 19:30), the break-through into incarnate spiritual relationships in the Church.

With the sending of the Spirit, believers are empowered to have the same intimate relationship with the Father as Jesus. They now cry out "Abba" (Gal 4:6; Rom 8:15) and they also embody the presence of God for one another as "temples" of the Holy Spirit (1 Cor 6:19). Relationships among believers are so transformed that believers are seen actually to embody Christ (Mt 25:31-46; Acts 9:4-5) and to mediate the love of the Father which is alive in us through the Spirit (1 Jn 4:13-16; Rom 5:5). Nowhere in the OT is it ever said that one's brethren mediate the presence of God. Love of fellow Israelites was commanded by Yahweh, but it is never said that this love *was* loving Yahweh.[59] Now love of the brethren is better than cultic sacrifices (Mk 12:33), and reconciliation must precede any temple worship (Mt 5:23-24). By the one Spirit they are baptized into the one body (1 Cor 12:13), so that they become not just a community of believers in Christ but are actually seen as a new communal reality, the "Body of Christ," in which Christ himself grows to his fulness (Eph 4:13).[60]

This description of early Christian experience correlates very closely with our third, "incarnational" stage. It presupposes a centering in transcendent love (Christ is the center of their community, and disciples

[59] Mühlen develops this point in *Entsakralisierung*, pp. 299-310.

[60] Hans Küng treats this image as the third of his group of three: people of God, creation of the Spirit, Body of Christ; see *The Church* (New York, 1967) pp. 107-260. The three images correspond to the three stages of development I have outlined, but whereas I have suggested the Body of Christ image as the more developed and inclusive, Küng opts for the centrality of the People of God image. It may well be that our age requires such an emphasis—to return to our beginnings; for, as we shall see, any stage is incomplete if separated from its roots. However, I see the Body of Christ image, according to our analysis, as evolutionarily a more inclusive and developed stage of Church understanding. It presupposes the other stages, however, and without them can only appear as monolithic.

are seen in Christ[61]) and also a purification of self-centered attitudes to enter more fully into a reconciled community.[62] The heart of the process is a dying to oneself for the other and an entering more deeply into commitment to Christ and the community that embodies him.[63]

This stage itself, however, is not enough. Just as Christ's death was not just for his disciples but for the whole world, so the disciples are empowered by the same Spirit and thus called to witness God's love to the world. The communal "incarnational" stage, therefore, must break out into what might be called a fourth, "eschatological" stage. Luke brings both aspects together.[64] For example, his description of Pentecost shows not only the forming of a sharing community but also the "release of power" of the Spirit for the apostles to preach boldly the good news of Christ. Community and mission reinforce each other, the one providing the worshiping base that calls down the power of the Spirit in the apostles, and the mission motivating a deepening Christian community (see Acts 4:23–31). John's view seems very much like Luke's; the very message is their love for one another (Jn 13:35). In principle, this mission will end only when the full number of believers is brought into oneness with Christ: "that all may be one" (Jn 17:20 f.).[65] Thus, as in the fourth stage of our schema, communal love in the Spirit gives rise to outgoing love, which in turn intensifies the communal love in an ever-expanding rhythm.

These, in broad outline, are biblical stages of spiritual growth that correspond to my developmental schema. The move from one stage to another was hardly ever smooth. Sin, understood as refusal of God's call to ongoing development, resisted the dying to self necessary to advance to the following stages.[66] Israel was moved from the clan stage only by the destruction of its center of institutional identity—Jerusalem and the Temple. And Judaism itself balked at going beyond its national limits to its universal mission in Christ. At each stage a dying was required: to corporate identity, then to spiritual individualism, then from communal worship to immersion in the world. Yet there was also fidelity to the past.

[61] See LaVerdiere and Thompson, *art. cit.* Luke especially focuses on Christ's presence among the disciples.

[62] *Ibid.* Matthew's rules for community emphasize this.

[63] As noted before (n. 21 above), the advice to the community is put in the context of the predictions of the Passion. Thus the whole of Christian life is seen as involving a dying to self.

[64] See LaVerdiere and Thompson, *art. cit.*

[65] See 1 Cor 15:24 for an even more universal expression of the mission of the Church, to bring all of creation into submission to Christ, and his final submission to the Father.

[66] Sin is here understood in relation to grace, and not simply as a moral fault. Hence, in a developmental view of the call of grace, sin will involve idolizing some present stage of development and refusing to open further to the transcendent call of grace.

Community was present in the end as in the beginning, and even more intensely, so that Christians could call themselves the "new Israel."[67] There is law in the end as in the beginning, but a "new covenant" law in the Spirit.[68] And there is a promise as in the beginning, but now one that even death cannot overcome, of an eschatological, transcendent kingdom. My notion of development seems confirmed: succeeding stages include the previous and even bring them "to a fuller realization within a richer context."[69]

Finally, the constant dynamism behind each new stage is God's love, sovereignly free, faithful, universal, and formative of community, but this love is ever more fully realized in each succeeding stage. Thus, God's freeing freedom called Abraham *from* a nontranscendent culture to obey Him personally, and the law called for free obedience. The spiritual break-through freed further from collectivism to individual responsibility and universal vision. Christ moved this freedom into real relationships by his willingness to face dying to himself for others, and the gift of the Spirit frees believers to love unconditionally in the world as grounded in God's transcendent freedom. God's fidelity also moves from a conditioned fidelity, to an unconditional promise, to an incarnate fidelity in relationships, and finally to eschatological fulfilment in Christ. His universal love moves from a particular promise to Abraham that all nations would be blessed in Him, to a universal vision of His Lordship, to incarnation of this universality in Christ's cross/resurrection and the "new creation," and finally to world transformation. Lastly, the community itself is gathered, interiorized, embodied, and sent forth to bring all into the one fold.

To conclude this section, these stages have been developed from spiritual psychology, and their biblical confirmation shows that they are appropriate to reveal God's action in our spiritual growth. They are not just past history but an ever-recurrent developmental pattern. If the view presented is correct, we would have to conclude even now that succeeding stages cannot be fully developed without the preparation of preceding stages. A later stage may emerge early—as with a spiritual break-through in a disintegrated personality—but one would have to take care that the preparatory stages are repaired if the succeeding ones are to yield their full fruit. Service to the world would then be seen as impotent or only feebly possible without a powerful spiritual community. Community would be impotent without reliance on the break-through of

---

[67] See Küng, *The Church*, pp. 68–69.

[68] I have already adverted to Luke's presentation of Pentecost as a new Sinai experience. Matthew makes a similar point by his interiorization of the law in his Sermon on the Mount (Mt 5–7).

[69] Lonergan, *Method in Theology*, p. 241.

the Spirit and the freedom of individual commitment, and that
break-through itself as disintegrating unless grounded in basic human
communities. The constant dynamism behind every stage of development would be God's love, and the gift of community-forming Spirit.

WHY, THEN, THE CHURCH?

I began with the question, in a world where anonymous Christianity is
a real possibility, "Why the Church?" I insisted that the usual norm for
discovering the working of the Spirit and hence salvation is selfless love.
Admitting that selfless love is a sign of God's love, since it is only possible
on the basis of a transcendent ground, the question still addressed us:
What then is God's love, when is love really selfless? My argument has
been that fully selfless love is only manifested in the cross/resurrection of
Jesus, that this event is normative for selfless love wherever it occurs.
Further, I argued that the cross reveals four qualities of such divine love:
freedom, fidelity, universality, and community-forming. Not only that,
but since the cross/resurrection is no isolated event but the culmination
of a people's divine formation and preparation, it can only be interpreted
historically as culminating stages of historical development: of community, reliance on divine power, and the unification of these in the
spiritual community that was the early Church. And even this Church is
not in itself sufficient to manifest God's love unless it is moved out by the
very divine power within it to manifest God's universal community-forming love and co-operate with the movements of the Spirit in the world.
What would such a position say to the question "Why the Church?"

In the first place, it would have to criticize a one-sided view of the
Church as primarily a servant of the world; for the mission aspect of the
Church in the above view is to manifest God's love as revealed in the
cross/resurrection event, much as is presented in Matthew's Gospel, and
that event does not stand alone but is the culmination of a whole history
of community formation which enters into the content of the mission.
The spiritual community of the Church is itself the message—the
effective revelation of God's love in the world as a possibility of human
development.[70] Only if the Church converts to becoming a living
manifestation of God's love will it be a real embodiment of the message of
the kingdom. This seems to me the theological reason why efforts at
social transformation have proved unavailing: the lack of spiritual
community supporting them; for it is not just individual acts of selfless

---

[70] This view does not take away from the need for mission, and for adapting to the needs
of the people one serves and their stage of development (as Haight argues, *art. cit.*). But if
this service is to go beyond helping people be healed for the first of our stages, it will involve
further conversion and development of community in the Church. One cannot give what
one does not have.

love that it is the mission of the Church to communicate, but community-forming, committed love, and this can be communicated only if it is
really being lived.

Secondly, it would also be insufficient to the question "Why the
Church?" to say simply that it was to form a community of faith in Jesus
Christ; for this would make the community center solely on its relation to
Jesus and to one another, and would not go beyond itself, as Jesus
himself did, to reveal the universality of his Father's love. This would be
equivalent to an exclusivist ecclesiology and would not be taking
seriously the reality of God's grace outside the boundaries of the
believing community.[71]

Thirdly, however, could we not simply hold a representational
ecclesiology, accepting the reality of grace outside the boundaries of the
Church and affirming that the Church was there to show what was
basically possible independent of its witness? It is difficult to exclude
this possibility in theory, given the possibility of grace outside the
Church, but it does seem highly unlikely, given some reflection on our
experience. One likely candidate as revelation of God's grace, for
example, would be the high points of Eastern spirituality. There
certainly we have the recognition of oneness, of the need to die to egoism,
and of compassionate concern for suffering humanity. However, if our
analysis of Trinitarian love is taken as norm, that love would fall short
precisely through its absence of community-forming thrust. The Eastern
view of God is monistic, so that community could not be considered as a
transcendent goal—perhaps as a means, but not as itself a glimmering of
the divine community that is our future. Hence that revelation would be
more in line with the second stage of my historical analysis—from
collectivism to spiritual universal individualism—and not a manifestation of the fulness of Trinitarian love.

Could we not point to a political movement such as Marxism,
therefore, as an example of selfless commitment to a just society where
each is respected for what he/she can give and helped for what he/she
needs? This does exemplify the community aspect of God's love, but falls
short of the norm of the cross/resurrection by its limiting its vision to this
world. God's Triune love is indeed a power for healing and love in this
world, as we have seen in my third stage, but its motivating power and
final vision is not this world but an opening to the transcendent power of
God's Spirit.

Perhaps, then, one could point to the good people one meets in

---

[71] See P. J. Schineller, "Christ and the Church: A Spectrum of Understandings," earlier
in this issue, for a description of this position. Matthew could hold this in an age when the
"world" was seen as much smaller; see LaVerdiere and Thompson, art. cit.

everyday life, people whose selfless love seems far superior to one's own, and who seem far better carriers of divine life than oneself. Apart from my early critique of such manifestations of selfless love (which may or may not be borne out in the long run), such individual acts may qualify an individual for divine life, but one could hardly say they manifested the quality of universality and community-forming that are needed to embody the fulness of God's love. If one is simply looking to individual salvation, then the question of the Church would seem not to arise at all. But if the Church is God's instrument to effectively manifest His own love in the world, then it needs a community base that lives from His Triune love.

Why, then, the Church? The answer the above position points to is that the Church is the normative and constitutive[72] embodiment of the fulness of Trinitarian love in the world, called to realize this love in itself and to co-operate with the movements of grace in the world according to its own experienced knowledge of the community components that enter into that love. It presupposes that Christ's death/resurrection established in the world a new possibility of spiritual community through the sending of the Spirit, and that this Trinitarian love is fully revealed only through such a community and the mission that springs from it. This would be predominantly a developmental schema, with a strong condition-intervention component, especially at the points of transition between stages.[73] It adds to Gregory of Nyssa's view, however, the communitarian focus of Augustine's pneumatology; for in my view the Church is not just a pedagogue of individuals in their process of purification (as necessary as this is) but precisely the locus of God's community-forming Spirit in whose power each member is opened to communal freedom, universality, and self-giving. One is educated precisely by being ever more deeply incorporated into the Body of Christ, and it would be this inspiriting that empowers the Church's action in the world. Because of the equal emphasis of community and mission in this view, it is more akin to the Lukan than the Matthean model. Both Christian community and mission are viewed as equally primary; for the mission is for the sake of expanding community, and the community for the sake of expanding mission.

Thus the Church would have a twofold task: to purify itself to become an embodiment of God's living Spirit, and to witness this love in the world and call the world's own manifestations of the Spirit to the fulness of Christian communal love. This is well expressed by Rosemary

[72] Schineller, art. cit., for a description of this type of ecclesiology. The difference between this ecclesiology and that of Karl Rahner lies not in the type but in the interpersonal ontology that underlies it; see n. 24 above.

[73] See Burns, art. cit., for a development of the implications of these two options.

Haughton in a recent book:

The Christian community has two tasks, which are not separable but are distinct. . . . The community has to organize itself, and organize with others, in order to bring to bear on its own worldly situation the understanding it gains in its calling. This is its task of religion-making. But in order to do this truly, and make a religion which can worship God and not idols, it must also come into being as a community made not by hands, but by the act of God. This act is an act of judgement, and it is by undergoing this judgement that the community exists as spiritual. By this also it is enabled both to *be* and to *utter* God's judgement on the world, which includes its own worldly building. . . . *Only* the Spirit can do this, when he acts in people and sets them free to love each other.[74]

Thus the Church has itself to hear the call of divine love to conversion and spiritual community, and from this basis of experience to witness to God's call to the world. It may well be that the Church is predominantly in the first stage of institutionalism and needs first to hear the prophetic call to convert and trust in God's transcendent love before it can gain the strength it needs to be sent out in joy. It need not postpone mission till this is done, since the stages mutually help one another, such that mission can be a strong motivation to become formed in spiritual community, as it was for the *Post American* community.[75] It would only mean that if the mission is truly to bring God's love, it must have as ground a living experience of that love in community. That experience, in the view here presented, involves the four stages of development, each of which needs renewal if the Church's witness is to be solid. Thus we are led to the following suggestions for renewal.

First, there needs to be renewed, or even formed, the familial basis, which heals emotional relationships and schools freedom to break loose from the collectivities of our world to find one's true self. Without that base the anxiety to secure one's place in our threatened world will prevent our hearing God's new call to grow. Israel had this component in her family feasts and community synagogues. Temple celebrations presupposed that familial base. This base is increasingly lost in our day when families are more and more uprooted in our "future shock" economy, and collectivism and individualism pervade our disintegrated neighborhoods and commercialized entertainment. If God is to build community on a natural base, we need to develop communities that neither our culture nor our Church as institution at present builds.[76]

---

[74] Rosemary Haughton, *The Theology of Experience* (New York, 1972) p. 58.

[75] See n. 17 above and the corresponding text.

[76] The strategy of developing "basic communities" in South America, and the trend to forming "covenant communities" in the charismatic renewal, both seem to be responding to this felt need.

Secondly, today, when we recognize better our human inadequacy, there needs to be renewed conviction that not Church structures, however necessary they be, nor merely human efforts, which also are needed, but God's community-forming love assures the Church's unity, existence, and growth. Israel's own institutions were razed in order for her to open to Yahweh's power for new creation. The remedy today, I hope, will not be as drastic, but it remains true that the Church today as before requires the same transcendent help for every aspect of renewal, from updating of liturgy to reinterpreting ministries. The charismatic renewal is only one instance of such a spiritual awakening in the Church,[77] but the trend must reach to seminaries and parishes if we are to move beyond a merely institutional communitarian life.

Thirdly, the Church needs the foundation of a strong spiritual community to empower mission. In the early Church Christ's cross/resurrection was the model for such healing and the unconditional forgiveness it implied. At Pentecost dispersed Jews were regathered by the Spirit, and the disciples were sent out with that message of reconciliation. The same is true today. The Church needs to heal divisions within our own communities and between Christian churches. There is but one Spirit, so our divisions must be seen as sinful (regardless of who was or is at fault). The cross/resurrection teaches that healing comes not from our own unaided efforts but from openness to God's reconciling love, which involves dying to our own (or the Church's) narrow self-justification or even self-condemnation, and opening to the unity God is effecting. If we open to Christ in our community (as was Luke's vision), we can emerge from our narrowness into the new unity to which we are called in the one Spirit.[78]

Fourthly, God's love in Jesus' cross was not just for the renewal of Israel: it is a universal call to repentance for the whole world. There is only one goal for the world, God's Triune love, and grace is everywhere at work. Hence the Church must bring its knowledge of spiritual community into ongoing dialogue with the world. It is not a one-way dialogue but a willingness to learn (as is clear from Roger Haight's

[77] Other examples are the renewal of Ignatian *Spiritual Exercises*, new methods of communal discernment, and the Cursillo movement, among others. The contagion of such movements as that of the Rev. Sun Myung Moon (See *Time*, June 14, 1976, pp. 48–50) and transcendental meditation shows the hunger of our age for transcendent experience. The Church is particularly called to embody a healthy openness to this dimension, which will help free people to creative community rather than enslave them.

[78] Heribert Mühlen has recently argued for a universal ecumenical council of all Christian churches, on the grounds that there is only one Spirit we all share by baptism, and we need to presuppose this unity in our efforts to embody it; see "Steps toward a Universal Council of Christians," *Theology Digest* 21 (1973) 196–201. The argument of this article would support his conclusion, provided, of course, we have broken through to the transcendent ground that we have seen is implied in such a reconciliation.

article) as well as critique. Thus it can learn from the Marxist concern for justice and the oppressed to recall its own early community experience.[79] Or it can learn from the Freudian exposé of our unconscious sinfulness to take seriously the prophetic challenge of Christ himself. On the other hand, it will judge the world's narrow nationalism (or its own narrow institutionalism) or the economic world's psychological manipulation (as well as its own administrative manipulation) that reveals an absolutizing of world structures and a closedness to God's transcendence. In constant openness to such learning and critique, the Church will transform itself and witness to the world according to God's love that it lives from.

CONCLUSION

I began with the question that anonymous Christianity presents to the Church. From the view here presented, God's love forms an enduring and committed community in the Spirit; it is not just the ground of individual acts of selfless love. It has been argued that committed community is essential if social structures, and not just individuals, are to be transformed by God's love. Such transformation is no mere structural change—which could be accomplished by separate acts of love—but a move to "new being," a committed, Spirit-empowered community of love. Anonymous Christianity cannot mean a negation of the necessity of such a spiritual community if it is not to divest the Church of its power so to transform structures. This article does not deny the possibility of such spiritual communities elsewhere in the world (though experience does not show this as likely), but only cautions that such a committed love, even beyond death, is no mere instance of selfless love but a life devoted to a transcendent love even at the cost of one's life.

"Why the Church?" Our response is: to become a living witness to this Trinitarian love. It is a vision that involves an ongoing conversion toward the freedom, fidelity, universality, and spiritual community that are revealed and effected by Christ's cross. The cross itself is the final manifestation of the inadequacy of any finite representation of this divine love, so that only by an ongoing dying to its finite values, immobile self-justification, and limited love will the Church, by extrapolation, reveal its source of life within, yet beyond, itself, the call of Trinitarian love which is the final goal of all the world. The Church must be a place where such a call to conversion is ever heard as both a judgment and a gift to itself and the world.

[79] Because of grace in the world, the world can and should be a call to the Church to recognize values it has neglected. However, if the Church is to grow in self-determination, it will look for the roots of these values in its own faith. We need, in the words of Archbishop Helder Camara of Brazil, a new Thomas Aquinas, who will do for Marxism what Thomas himself did for Aristotelianism (talk given at the University of Chicago at the celebration of our medieval heritage, November 1974).

COMMENTS ON ROBERT T. SEARS'S ARTICLE

After rereading Robert Sears's "Trinitarian Love as the Ground of the Church," I wished it had preceded my own instead of following it, since its position makes it appear as a retort or an alternative view. But this would obscure the fact that we share many common concerns and that I feel myself in agreement with most of his assertions, if not with his method. For example, he raises the question of the *kind* of love that is salvific and responds to it in clear and distinctly Christian terms. Thus I believe that our views could be taken as being complementary on a certain level, even while on another they are fundamentally different. I shall, therefore, briefly outline my position in his terms to show where we might agree and then try to pinpoint where we differ.

The point at issue lies in whether the *raison d'être* of the Church consists in its being a Christian community which also has a mission, or its being a Christian community-primarily-in-service-to-the-world.[1] Were I to adopt Sears's developmental point of view, I would insist more consistently than he does that, in Lonergan's words quoted by him, the final stage of religious development to which the Church is called is indeed a higher stage which "introduces something new and distinct, puts everything on a new basis, yet so far from interfering with the sublated or destroying it, on the contrary needs it, includes it, preserves all its proper features and properties, and carries them forward to a fuller realization within a richer context." Thus, to view the Church simply as a community of love and reconciliation (the third level) "is not enough"; this must be transcended in such a way that "communal love in the Spirit gives rise to outgoing love," a transition that requires a quantum jump (a "dying") "from communal worship to immersion in the world." Thus the Church, which *is* a spiritual community, is "raised to a higher realization" in a mission Church. The idea and the actual status of the Church as mission "develop more richly what was begun in previous stages." This new and richer context of existing and understanding includes the former stages, cannot exist authentically without them, and is nourished by them.[2] And yet this is a different and higher level of existing to which the Church is called, negatively because falling back to a prior stage or idolizing it "and refusing to open further to the transcendent call of grace" may involve sin, positively because in a Church whose mission is turned outward to the world God's "love is . . . more fully realized." In all this we agree.

The position of Sears, however, is quite different from this, because in reality, I believe, he is operating within the context of three stages of development and not four, having collapsed the third and fourth stages into a single one. Or else the goals, finalities, or intelligibilities of each of the higher stages are not distinguished in importance or are equally primary. Thus, he states that "both Christian community and mission are viewed as equally primary, for the mission is for the sake of expanding community, and the community for the sake of expanding mission." The strictly reciprocal or mutual interdependency between

[1] For my part, I hesitate to use Sears's phrase "servant of the world" because of its over-close association with that particular movement called "secular theology."
[2] I therefore agree with Sears that "service to the world would then be seen as impotent or only feebly possible without a spiritual community."

community (third stage) and outward-turned mission (fourth stage) on a *de facto* psychological and everyday level (which I accept) is raised by Sears to the level of understanding the very purpose or ultimate finality of the Church. It is here that we differ.

The reasons for this difference are multiple, but two stand out. The first, which is more fundamental and complicated and therefore cannot be dealt with adequately here, has to do with method. Sears, who begins his argument from above, from Scripture as an external and objective authority and from a dogmatic theological understanding of divine Trinitarian love, sees things from a different perspective than myself, since I assume a concrete, historical, and existential point of view and seek to correlate Christian symbols with a critical appreciation of the present situation both inside and outside the Church. Secondly, this difference in method, it seems, is implicit in a different understanding of the very word "Church." In Sears the term "Church" is eschatological, in the sense that it applies equally to the empirical Church and the final spiritual community. For this reason "the spiritual community of the Church is itself the message" of the Church, community tends to become an end in itself, and the goal of the Church of this world is the same Church in the end time. For my part, I prefer to limit the term "Church" to the community we see in this world and apply the symbol "kingdom of God" to the eschatological community.[3]

In sum, then, although I agree that the Church *is* a spiritual community, and although Sears too asserts that this community has an exigency for mission to the world, I cannot affirm that these are equally the finalities of the Church we know today. It appears to me impossible at this moment in time to assert that the goal of the Church is to draw all men and women into itself.[4] This would constitute the ultimate theological justification for triumphalism. And such an understanding would never allow any given church to sacrifice or even to risk its empirical existence as church (community) to its mission (or to the *missio Dei*) as sign for other people and of self-sacrificing love after Christ. Unless the Church passes to

---

[3] There are grounds in the New Testament for an eschatological understanding of the term "Church" (See Dulles' *Models of the Church*), but this usage can lead to an idealized language about the Church that is uncritical and unbelievable, as well as to a confusion about what exactly is being referred to by the word "Church." I find this ambiguity in Sears's article. For example, he writes that "the Church is the normative and constitutive embodiment of the fulness of Trinitarian love in the world." But since in his view there is salvation outside the visible Church, and other authentic spiritual communities may exist, relative to salvation the Church is *not* constitutive but normative and representational. Or, since the Church is also the final community sharing Trinitarian love, in which the Church community in this world already shares proleptically and consciously, then the Church in this world *is* constitutive of salvation by participation. Or, since the Church in this world is constitutive of salvation, and since there is salvation and may be authentic spiritual community outside this Church, where these latter occur, there too is the Church. Or, finally, all of these positions might be affirmed at once. These ambiguities could be easily cleared up by restricting the word "Church" to the visible Christian communities we see.

[4] Lack of space prevents development of the positive theological justification for this position, which has been worked out in mission theology.

Sears's fourth stage, where the spiritual community is precisely not primarily in service of itself, the Church will not be a credible witness to the divine love manifested in the cross of Jesus.

ROGER D. HAIGHT, S.J.